Devotional Companion

to the

International Lessons
2004–2005

Usable with All Popular Lesson Annuals

Jeffrey A. Rasche

ABINGDON PRESS / Nashville

DEVOTIONAL COMPANION TO THE INTERNATIONAL LESSONS 2004–2005

Copyright © 2004 by Abingdon Press

This book is printed on acid-free paper.

ISBN 0-687-07460-6
ISSN 1074-9918

04 05 06 07 08 09 10 11 12 13 — 10 9 8 7 6 5 4 3 2 1

MANUFACTURED IN THE UNITED STATES OF AMERICA

Hymnals Referenced

B   Forbis, Wesley, ed. *The Baptist Hymnal*. Nashville: Convention Press, 1991.

C   *The Cokesbury Worship Hymnal*. Nashville: Abingdon Press, 1966.

E   Glover, Raymond, ed. *The Hymnal 1982*. New York: The Church Hymnal Corporation, 1985.

F   Bock, Fred, ed. *Hymns for the Family of God*. Nashville: Paragon Associates, Inc., 1976.

L   *Lutheran Book of Worship*. Minneapolis: Augsburg Publishing House, 1978.

P   McKim, LindaJo, ed. *The Presbyterian Hymnal*. Louisville: Westminster/John Knox Press, 1990.

UM   Young, Carlton R., ed. *The United Methodist Hymnal*. Nashville: The United Methodist Publishing House, 1989.

W   Batastini, Robert J., ed. *Worship*. Chicago: GIA Publications, 1986.

READ IN YOUR BIBLE: *Psalm 150*   **September 5, 2004**
SUGGESTED PSALM: *Psalm 100*
SUGGESTED HYMNS:
  "Holy, Holy, Holy" (All)
  "Thine Be the Glory" (B, F, L, P, UM)

Discovering Our Value in God's Creation

Hearing the Word

Have you ever felt happy just to be alive? Have you ever paused to realize what a miracle it is to have all the blessings you have? Psalm 150 is one of many psalms written to capture that feeling and express it in worship. For the Jewish people worship was not all about asking God for things; it was about recognizing God for all that God has done, and giving God thanks. The phrase "supreme greatness" reminds us of the first commandment, especially in a culture where there were other religions claiming other gods to be great. Our God is real, our God is supreme.

Living the Word

At a recent gathering of numerous churches in our area, an elderly man sat next to me and quietly read the bulletin. The first item in the bulletin was "Praise Music." He turned to me, holding a hymnal, and asked if I knew what page the music was on. Before I could answer him, a "contemporary band" took the stage to lead worship. With a blast from the amplifiers, the drummer began beating on the trap set. Suddenly the video screens overhead flickered to life. "I think the words are going to be on the screens," I told my neighbor. He persisted in holding the hymnal, and looking in the bulletin for more information. About that time a young man seized the microphone and shouted, "We are here to praise God!" People applauded, like at a concert; and with that, the young man began to sing the words that were on the screen. Several people, including a young woman in front of us, jumped to their feet and began to sing, clap, and dance to the beat. The more she danced and sang and lifted her hands to a song she obviously knew and loved, the more it was painfully apparent that the elderly man not only had never heard this song but was uncomfortable with clapping or dancing in church. He began to frown. "I don't like this kind of music," he said. "It's so loud, you can't hear yourself think. It's not traditional!"

The service was just too different for the elderly man to feel comfortable. However, I thought his comment that it wasn't "traditional" shows that he has not read Psalm 150 lately. "Praise him with trumpets . . . with drums and dancing . . . with loud cymbals." Apparently, loud praise music with instruments was the tradition.

However, Psalm 150 also lists harps and flutes. These are quiet, peaceful instruments. They are great background for prayer and meditation; they have a beauty and dignity that loud, clashing cymbals lack.

Perhaps Psalm 150 is saying there are many different ways to praise God and that all of them are important. Some people do not feel like they have praised God unless they have clapped and cheered and waved their arms while listening to a band. On the other hand, some people prefer a more reserved way; they see beauty in the subtle voice of the flute or harp that they do not hear in the loud cymbals. And if some of us danced like that young woman who was in front of us danced, we would have to visit a chiropractor on Monday.

Maybe in this day of contemporary and traditional worship, we need to reexamine Psalm 150. There are different, and equally meaningful, ways to praise God. If you like the loud cymbals, praise God with them. If you are moved by the quiet poetic melodies of the harp or flute, praise God with them. You non-dancers, loosen up and clap a little. It won't kill you. And you who sing from the video screens, learn to appreciate the depth of meaning found in the quiet music in the hymnal, too. Let us together praise our God, who made us all.

Let us pray:
Lord, help us praise you in our worship, and express our gratitude to you every day of our life. Whether we use the loud cymbals or the quiet harp, may our heart and deeds say "Thank you for life, thank you for one another, and thank you for being who you are." Amen.

Beginning Again

Hearing the Word

The story of Noah and the Flood helps to set the stage for the rest of the Bible. The basic problem, introduced earlier in Genesis, is sin: the disobedience of the humans whom God created to be good but who chose (choose) evil over good. The flood was God's attempt to eliminate the problem of sin by ending the life of sinners and saving the one family that was good—Noah's. However, this meant a level of destruction and death that proved unacceptable to God, particularly when Noah and Noah's sons turned out to be infected with the sin virus too (see Genesis 9:18-29). Since it turned out that every human is sinful, God's covenant shows that God decided to lay down his weapons; he put his bow in the sky (Genesis 9:13). God resolved to find some other way to save us from our sins besides destroying sinners. The rest of the Bible could then profitably be understood as God's continuing struggle to win us back not by violence, but with love and trust.

Living the Word

A group of men were talking about the potential war with Iraq. At the time the threats of war were heating up to a fever pitch. Some were expressing opinions that included negative comments about Iraqis in general. A wise, older war veteran corrected them. "Hey," he scolded, "watch what you say about Iraqis. It won't be long until the war is over, and before you know it they will be our good friends."

One of the basic decisions we have to make in life is to figure out who is our enemy and who is our friend. So what about God—enemy or friend?

It is natural to reply that God is our friend. But sometimes it sounds

7

like we are not completely convinced. We have this sneaking suspicion that God, who laid down his weapon, who placed his bow in the sky, might snatch it back up again and open fire. Consider this example. A person says, "I can't believe someone committed a crime like that murder, and got away with it!" But another person replies, "Well, the person might have escaped, but someday God will get 'em." In other words, God becomes our warrior, sent to attack those sinners who hurt us but whom we can't get our hands on. In that case God would still be our personal friend, but we are wishing him on someone else as an enemy.

Consider another example. Sometimes in our guilt we wonder whether God will find a way to punish us for our sins. Just the thought that God punishes sinners must mean that at times God picks the bow back up out of the clouds; the peaceful rainbow is transformed into a horrific weapon of punishment, and sinners are the targets. Do you think that if you are a sinner this promise in Genesis 9:8-17 doesn't cover you anymore? (If there are any sinners reading this, and you don't see the rainbow in the sky at this moment, maybe you should run for cover.) How do you believe that God deals with sin, after all?

Others speak of God destroying the world someday, but they rule out flooding based on today's scripture. "God never said he would not destroy the world by fire or meteors or volcanic explosions or famine—he only said he would not destroy the world by flood." Now there is a comforting thought. God must have a clever lawyer to set up a contract with so many loopholes. My gosh, with even a little creativity, God could think of hundreds of fascinating ways to destroy us.

As for me, I think God truly decided way back then to be our friend. I don't think God used a lawyer in drawing up that covenant to create any loopholes. God was trying to tell us that he did not want to deal with sinners by destroying them. And ever since then God has been trying to find a way not to destroy sinners, but to save them—no, to save us. Yes, God is our friend—all the time. He laid his weapons down for good.

Let us pray:
Lord, thank you for being our friend. Help us live as your friend, and as a friend to all those you have made. Amen.

READ IN YOUR BIBLE: *Exodus 3:13-17*   **September 19, 2004**

SUGGESTED PSALM: *Psalm 8*

SUGGESTED HYMNS:

"*Holy God, We Praise Thy Name*" (E, F, L, P, UM, W)

"*O Worship the King*" (B, C, E, F, L, P, UM)

Power for Deliverance

Hearing the Word

In the English language, a noun is a person, place, or thing; a verb describes an action (to run, to jump, and so forth). The name of a person, such as Moses, is considered a noun. When Moses asked for God's name, the answer God gave him was the verb for "to be." The Hebrew name "Yahweh" sounds like the verb "to be," which is meaningful to describe God since it includes the forms "was," "is," "will be," "has always been," "will continue to be," "being," and "causes to be." It implies that God exists at all times, and God created everything that exists. It also implies that God is in action, and not merely an object.

Living the Word

A prospective student called the admissions office of a college. "I'm interested in your computer classes," he said.

The admissions officer said, "Oh, you're in luck. Our school has one of the greatest computer teachers anywhere in this whole part of the country. He is a well-known expert in his field, and has published several books that other schools use as textbooks. Not only that, he is just a great guy; he is as friendly and nice as any of our professors. He always has time to spend with students to help them with their work. You'll definitely have to meet him when you come for a campus tour. He's a fantastic teacher."

The potential student was excited. "That's great!" he said. "What's his name?"

At that, the admissions officer paused, embarrassed. "I'm sorry," she said, "but I'm not sure. I'll have to look it up. Let's see . . . I think it's listed in one of these books here. . . . Well, I can't find it; but really, he's an excellent teacher."

9

What is wrong with this picture? This admissions officer was sending a mixed signal. How can you think the world of a person but not remember his or her name?

Maybe this is why Moses wanted to know God's name. After all, how could he speak for God but not even know God's name? He would lose credibility in a hurry. It is like telling the IRS that the person you talked with on the phone last week said that you did not have to pay more taxes than you have already paid. So when asked "Who did you talk to?" if you say, "I don't know who the person was," then you may as well not have had the conversation. But if the person you name is the boss of the IRS employee you are talking to, then the name will carry a lot of weight.

So yes, Moses needed to know God's name to establish his credibility as God's spokesperson. But there is another reason that knowing the name is important; it is that God is interested in a personal relationship with us. I think of a conversation I once had with a person who has a Ph.D. I was introduced to the person as the Reverend Rasche, but I quickly said, "Hi, but please just call me Jeff." Then, when that person was introduced as Dr. Smith (I'll fictionalize the name), I made the mistake of venturing, "Should I just call you (by your first name)?" He coldly replied, "No, usually people address me as Dr. Smith." Obviously, we have never become fishin' buddies.

The thought that God would be interested in us on a personal level is really, if you think about it, amazing. After all, God is GOD! You know, the one who can speak a word, and all the oceans roll back and uncover the continents! God invented flight for butterflies and painted the delicate color of their wings. And it is this same God, whose titles are far more impressive than any Ph.D., who wants to swap names with you, to be your trusted friend.

Many of us, especially when we are introduced to several people at a time, forget the names as fast as we hear them. But there is one whose name is above all other names, and yet will never forget yours. Do you recall that name?

Let us pray:
Lord, thank you for wanting to know us personally, by name. Help us to remember you in all that we do, that we may live up to your holy name. Amen.

Becoming God's People

Hearing the Word

Today's devotional scripture is part of Moses' farewell address to the people of Israel as they are about to enter the promised land. By this time the people have received the Ten Commandments, and as they wandered the desert they have been transformed from a band of runaway slaves to a growing and organized nation. Moses is laying out their choices from God: either to obey God's commandments and live well in the promised land, or to disobey them and be destroyed. God rewards and punishes us for our obedience or disobedience.

Living the Word

A man and his wife purchased two four months old miniature donkeys. One of the donkeys was chocolate brown with light patches around her eyes, and the other white with gray patches. They were the first real "livestock" purchase the city-raised couple had ever made. In preparation, the couple had read several books about miniature donkeys and talked at length to various people who owned them or raised them. The couple had set up everything needed in a stall of the barn, and fenced in a pasture area connected to the stall for the donkeys to run and play in safety.

Just after Christmas, the couple pulled a livestock trailer to the donkey dealer who simply lifted/flopped the babies into the trailer. Suddenly these two animals, all of thirty inches tall, stood looking lost in that sixteen-foot horse trailer. The dealer shut the door, and the trip home began.

When the donkeys arrived home that cold winter day, the stall was warm and inviting, full of fresh hay, water, and food. The couple opened the trailer door and waited for the donkeys to step into their

11

new home. Instead, the animals just stood on the trailer, attentive but not moving. One man got into the trailer to shoo them out, but they simply ran circles around him, avoiding the opening like it was the Grand Canyon. He tried to pick one of them up, but it squirmed mightily; when one half came up, the other went down. When all four legs were in the air, they kicked about so frantically that the man realized this plan might move him from the bass to the soprano section in the church choir. Finally, with a piece of plywood, he got behind the donkeys and kept slowly moving them forward. Eventually they were standing next to the edge. There they simply stopped. They could not be pushed or scooted or budged.

At this point the women took over. They petted and cooed to the donkeys. They fed them treats, and then held the treats just out of reach across the threshold of the trailer. They laid down a plank with a trail of treats on it leading to the stall. The trailer was going to be their new and permanent home. Everyone gave up and went inside to have dinner and think about what to do next. Of course when the people went back out, the donkeys were standing in the stall, looking like they wondered what all the fuss was about.

In the scripture text, at this point in the story of the Israelites, they had been transported to the edge of the promised land. It was ready and waiting for them, but before they went in, Moses wanted them to remember that God had brought them there and that they needed to do God's will in the land. He used a carrot-and-stick approach much like those people used in trying to get the donkeys out of the trailer. He told them of the rewards of obedience to God, and the perils of disobedience. In forty years with them, he had learned that at times people can be as stubborn as those little donkeys were.

That has not changed even today. Why is it that people can know what is good for them, and see it spelled out in front of them, but resist it with all their might? Why is it that we need the promise of a reward, and maybe even the threat of punishment, to motivate us to do what is best for us? Silly creatures.

Let us pray:
Lord, thank you for the good things you have prepared for us. Help us open our eyes to your good and perfect will for us, and be obedient to your laws, which are designed to protect and enhance our life. Forgive us when we are so stubborn that we think our ways are better than yours. In Christ, Amen.

"*How Firm a Foundation*" *(All)*
"*Immortal, Invisible, God Only Wise*" *(B, E, F, L, P, UM, W)*

Leaving a Legacy

Hearing the Word

King David is known as one of Israel's greatest kings. That is why the Israelites expected the Messiah to be a descendant of his. Saul was the first king, but he was rejected by God and replaced by David. David was a beloved ruler who consolidated power in the kingdom and successfully kept all twelve tribes together. His son Solomon was the only other king to rule over the united tribes, which later split into the northern kingdom of Israel and the southern kingdom of Judah. Solomon ended up being the king who built the Temple, which was a major architectural feat for the day. When the kingdom was becoming stabilized under King David, it was natural for David to want to build a temple for God. It would have been not only a religious tribute but a popular and highly visible political achievement. He consulted God about the idea, and God let him know that it could wait.

Living the Word

On a mission trip to Louisiana with a youth group, we worked on a house that had been damaged by Hurricane Lily. The family escaped injury, but two huge trees had blown over on the roof, destroying their home. For a week twenty-two youth were busy hammering, framing up a house. To see it rise from the dirt was like a miracle. One day the beams were put on the foundation blocks, then the floor, and then the walls rose. By the last day the windows were in place, and we were putting rafters on the roof. As afternoon ended, clearly we were not going to finish even half of the roof. Our tremendous sense of accomplishment was frustrated as we walked away from the house that was still open to the rain.

Then we heard that another group was scheduled to come the next week to work on the roof. Although we would have loved to have stayed and finished the whole project ourselves, one group after another would come, building on each other's work to add drywall, electric work, plumbing, paint, cabinets, and flooring.

In the church, we are given the chance to make our mark, to accomplish something for God. But we are building on the work of others who have come before us; and before our work is truly complete, we will pass the baton on to others who follow us. Sometimes we expect to "arrive" when a step in the right direction is what we can realistically expect to accomplish. But what is wrong with a step in the right direction? It helps to remember that God is the one with the overall plans, and we are on God's team.

Lyle Schaller, a noted church-growth expert, once spoke of the AAEOL Club—"Angry, Alienated, Ex-Old-Leaders Club." He said this club could be found in many churches. It consists of people who used to run things in the church. Of course the new leaders have new ideas that don't square with the way the AAEOL Club members used to do things. So the club members get together in the church basement, their Sunday school class, or at the coffee shop and complain about the new ways.

If this sounds familiar, and you are in that club, maybe it is time to get out of it. Instead of resenting that the new leaders are doing things in a different way, remember that God is really the chief contractor; we are just steps in God's plan. Instead, feel honored to have been a part of the process. Feel proud of your accomplishments, of taking a step in the right direction in your time. Support the current church leaders with your prayers, enthusiasm, and genuine help when it is needed and appreciated. Remember that even King David did not accomplish everything in his day. He wanted to build God's temple, but it was his son, the younger generation, who had that opportunity to shine. And even that was just another step forward for God. For God always has a new step to take, a new foundation or floor or wall or roof to build upon the work of those who have come before, and as a beginning for those who will come later.

Let us pray:
Lord, thank you for the ways that you have, and still can, use me for your purposes. Help me to see and appreciate the many good things that have gone before that set the stage for opportunities to serve you now. Amen.

SUGGESTED PSALM: *Psalm 142*

SUGGESTED HYMNS:

 "O God, Our Help in Ages Past" (All)
 "Morning Has Broken" (B, E, F, P, UM, W)

Re-creating Community

Hearing the Word

Isaiah lived during the Jewish Exile in 586 B.C., when the Babylonians conquered what was left of the Jewish people living in the promised land. The first thirty-nine chapters of Isaiah warn of this event; but in chapter 40 and following, Isaiah offers words of hope and new direction to the people who are grieved and lost, without their land, without their temple, and without their social structure. Since the people had been soundly defeated by Babylon's military, Isaiah had a difficult task ahead of him to restore their confidence. In this section, he reminds them of God's powerful creativity to inspire their confidence in God; in a way it is like saying that even though Babylon seems overwhelmingly powerful, God is still more powerful. Therefore God is portrayed in verse 13 as a warrior, ready to go to battle on their behalf. Historically, that was not needed. When Cyrus of Persia came to power, he actually invited the Israelites to return to their homeland; eventually some did go.

Living the Word

It was a mid-sized article on the inside pages of a newspaper. Two teenagers were fishing on a river. One of them stood up in the boat, tripped on a tackle box, and fell out. He disappeared beneath the surface. His companion panicked and jumped in after him. By the time rescuers pulled the boys to the surface, it was too late. For the news, it was a bigger story because two young people drowned at one time.

For the boys' families you can imagine that the story was life-shattering. It would leave them devastated, and probably raise all kinds of questions about their faith. Where was God? Was this God's will? Why didn't God prevent it from happening? These are legitimate and

15

understandable questions for those who suffer such a tragic loss. It would be surprising if the families did not feel this way.

In a similar way, the Exile caused the Jewish people to question God. They had a lot of their family and friends killed in the battle; those who survived were taken prisoners of war and made to leave the promised land. Many of their leaders were killed, and the Temple was destroyed. The people were unable to continue their corporate life as a religious or political community. In a word, they were devastated. They felt that God had let them down, and they questioned God's will and/or God's ability to help them.

Then the prophet Isaiah began to offer them words of comfort and hope. He told them that God still had a purpose for them, and a plan to restore them to their land. He reassured them that God was still good and wanted the best for them. He helped them visualize a better and brighter future, and reminded them that God was indeed strong—strong enough to stand up and fight for them like a warrior.

Honestly, even though this is a beautiful vision, and the words of hope are great to hear, it does not satisfactorily answer all of the questions that the Exile (or other tragedies like the double drowning that summer) raises. Some of our questions simply must remain questions. They have no answers we can grasp at this time. It is frustrating, but probably it is worse to try to live with some false answer that is designed to make tragedy acceptable.

The part of the answer we can see and understand is that even tragedy does not stop God who still has an answer, a healing alternative, another "card to play." Our God is never defeated by the most unthinkable tragedy. This is not to say that it is ever easy for the people who live the story. And it is not to say that their questions, their doubts, their anger, are inappropriate. But surely God understands that, too. Even in the midst of tragedy, God continues to dream, to bring hope, and to do a new thing.

Let us pray:
Lord, please be with those who grieve today, and those who have experienced tragedy in their life. Help us to show our love and compassion to those who suffer such devastating losses. Even though we do not understand, help us to hear others' questions and ask our own questions, and to wrestle with the answers in the context of knowing that somewhere, somehow, you are still there with us, hoping for and working for the best. Amen.

READ IN YOUR BIBLE: *Jeremiah 30:18-22*   **October 17, 2004**
SUGGESTED PSALM: *Psalm 147*
SUGGESTED HYMNS:
 "This Is My Father's World" (B, C, E, F, L, P, UM)
 "There Is a Balm in Gilead" (B, E, F, P, UM, W)

Creating a New Covenant

Hearing the Word

The Exile could be understood as the "death" of Israel, for Israel was created by God's promise to Abraham and God's desire to be in covenant relationship with the Israelites. The promise to Abraham was twofold: a land in which to live (promised land), and numerous descendants. While the people were faithful to God, they were being led to the promised land (or sustained in it), and they were growing in numbers. The violence of the Exile reduced the number of people, and it evicted the survivors from the promised land; it also seemed that the covenant relationship with God was broken because the Temple was destroyed and all semblance of national order was disrupted. Therefore these few reassuring verses of Jeremiah could be considered a resurrection of sorts. In them God expresses a desire to renew the covenant relationship with the Israelites, restore them to their land, and increase their numbers.

Living the Word

Scientists believe that throughout the earth's history there have been several mass extinctions of species. The cause(s) of these events are uncertain. Some scientists attempt to correlate them with giant meteor strikes that would have thrown so much debris into the atmosphere that the weather patterns all over the planet would have dramatically changed for years, eliminating normal food supplies and resulting in the extinction of many species at one time (of course roaches have made it through it all). Other scientists think that a series of massive volcanic eruptions may be the culprit. There are other theories too, but who really knows for sure? In any case, according to the fossil record, it appears that there have been several different types of species on earth. Each one (except humans so far) has eventually faced calamity and been almost completely wiped out. Then, over time, more and different types of creatures populated the earth again, all the way up until the next mass extinction.

Now this is not the place to debate the religious or scientific merit of evolution, though it is important to understand what Scripture tells us about God as the creator, and to understand that scientists are constantly proposing, then debating, and often later rejecting various theories. Usually I find that the more they describe about the wonders and mysteries of this great planet, the more I stand in awe of what God has done and how miraculous it all is. For evolution to have created the incredible biodiversity that we currently have on the planet, let alone to do it over and over again after setbacks like major meteor strikes, and particularly to do so randomly without God, is a little like saying that a meteor hit a junkyard, and when all the pieces came tumbling down out of the sky they somehow landed in such a way that they formed a whole parking lot of complete, polished, shiny new automobiles, with headlights in place and working.

In other words, to the extent that scientists are right in describing the past, I still believe that God was the creator behind it all; to me to not believe that is irrational and illogical. That kind of creativity is more than random luck. Again and again it happened, and each time the chaos was restored to order. It's no accident of nature.

Essentially, this is the faith that Jeremiah is preaching when he tells the Israelites, after the Exile, that they will be restored to their land and remade into a new community. He believes in a God who is able to restore, to make all things new. It makes you wonder whether this same God can work in our lives that way too. If God can respond to a massive meteor strike or world-changing volcanic eruption as a way to create a whole new world, then surely we can trust God with our problems. God is able to make all things new. Always!

Let us pray:
Lord, we are temporary, but you last forever. Help us put our faith and hope in you, and trust you with the problems we have that threaten us. Through Christ our Lord, Amen.

SUGGESTED HYMNS:
  "In Christ There Is No East or West" (All)
  "Let Us Break Bread Together" (B, E, F, L, P, UM, W)

Looking for Hope

Hearing the Word

Today both the lesson scripture and devotional scripture come from Ezekiel 37, but they are from two different visions. The lesson scripture is the famous "valley of dry bones" vision. Behind the eerie vision of dead bones clanking together and coming back to life is a message of hope for a people who feel as dead and dried out as those bones. It is this hope that links that vision to the devotional text later in the chapter. Using the object lesson of the two sticks held end to end to appear as one, God instructs Ezekiel to give people hope that they will once again live under a single rule with God's blessing.

Living the Word

One morning a young man delivered a load of lumber, so we worked together to carry it inside. Having the common goal of moving all that lumber, and needing each other to do it, created an ideal time to talk about Christian faith. I learned that his church did not allow him to own a car unless it was painted black; my cars are bright colors. He wore suspenders because his church did not permit belts; but in mine you don't need to wear suspenders unless you've been to too many potlucks. In spite of our obvious differences, we had similar beliefs about the "core" Christian beliefs and mission.

One fascinating practice of his church was that they did not do anything unless they had perfect agreement. If even one person opposed an idea, then they would continue to discuss it until all agreed. By contrast, our church is ruled by a simple majority on most matters. I asked him what they did if one person refused to agree with what everyone else felt was reasonable; I wondered if it would too easily prevent the church from doing its work. He questioned how we could proceed with an idea if numerous people in the church opposed it. He was concerned that it would threaten the unity of the church (of course sometimes it does).

We did not try to convert the other person to our views; instead, as we parted company, he smiled broadly, shook my hand, and said, "It was good to talk, even if we don't agree on everything."

It is a good thing to talk to people who believe differently than we do, and still respect them. There are too many occasions where our religious differences become a barrier between us. Too easily we allow ourselves to become like the two separate sticks that Ezekiel was instructed to hold up; we are too willing to part company, to divide the church, to vilify others who disagree with us.

Happily there are many refreshing examples to the contrary; these Ezekiel symbolized by two sticks held together in the hand as one. For example, there are many interdenominational clergy groups that meet regularly, and many churches of different denominations that work together.

It can be threatening to listen to someone we do not agree with. After all, they might actually make sense if we give them the chance to prove that they are not crazy for having an opinion different from our own. It takes someone who is secure in his or her faith to be able to hear out another person with respect.

I confess that I was intrigued by my friend's idea that the church should keep talking, even to a minority of one, until it reaches complete agreement. It sounds idealistic, like Ezekiel's vision of a future, undivided kingdom of God's people. The good thing about my friend's church's way is that they have to keep talking to those who disagree with them; they keep talking in spite of their differences.

We all can learn from that. If we treat others with respect and seek ways to work together, then it is easy for God's hands to hold all of us. Suspenders or belts, black cars or green ones, when we work together and respect each other, in Christ we all can be one.

Let us pray:
Lord, forgive us for judging others harshly and failing to listen and talk to one another. Help us who are different in many ways to become one in your hands, not by expecting others to become our carbon copies, but by respecting each other and working together. Through Christ we pray for unity in the church, Amen.

Creating a Renewed Trust

Hearing the Word

The person who wrote Psalm 91 and the person who wrote Psalm 73 (today's devotional and lesson scriptures, respectively) both believed in God as a protector of those who are faithful. Psalm 73 wrestles more with the problem of those occasions when evil people prosper and good people suffer. These psalms express a common theology in the Old Testament, namely that God rewards the faithful and punishes the wicked in the events of this life. It is important to know that there are other Old Testament writers who questioned why evil people sometimes prosper, while good people sometimes suffer (see especially Ecclesiastes and Job).

Living the Word

Not long ago, as I was driving along a gravel road, numerous black birds on it flew away as my car approached. But I noticed one bird up ahead standing in the middle of the road. I thought it too would fly. However, as I reached the point at which the bird had to fly to avoid being hit, it still had not spread its wings. Quickly I hit the brakes and skidded on the gravel. I hoped that my last-minute effort was enough, but when I looked in my rearview mirror, the bird lay dead on the road.

I felt a little heartsick. I love animals, so I kicked myself all the rest of the way home for simply running over that bird—why didn't I just slow down sooner? I tried to tell myself that all the other birds had flown away in good time, and that if I had stopped for all of them it would have taken an hour to drive five miles. Perhaps the bird was too sick to fly—who knows? I just felt guilty.

That is why, two days later, I wondered about the justice of God.

I was sitting with my wife on a Sunday afternoon on a bench next to our small backyard pond. It is a peaceful, serene spot. It is mesmerizing to watch the goldfish swim around, and hear the waterfall splash down the rocks and into the water.

Suddenly, though, the calm was interrupted when I felt something hit my arm. I looked down, and it was nasty bird mess. As I went inside to clean up, I suddenly remembered the bird I hit on the gravel road and wondered if there was any connection. If so, I thought I got off pretty easily, really, for hitting a poor little bird with my car.

Now, I'm half kidding here in linking these two true stories; but the half that is not kidding invites you to consider the theological implications. What is the connection between our sins and the subsequent events of our lives? Would you affirm that God was mad at me for not slowing down enough on the gravel road and therefore, two days later when I was feeling happy and peaceful, dispatched a bird that had just stuffed itself at the blackberry patch to bomb me? Or, do you think that I was merely sitting in the wrong place at the wrong time?

For centuries people have asked this theological question: Should we understand the bad events of this life as God's punishment for the wicked, and should we understand the good events as God's reward for the righteous?

Don't answer too quickly! Great minds in the Bible struggled to understand this question; today's psalmist poetically expressed his belief that God will cover the righteous with "God's wings" of protection. We must hold this idea of the way God works in creative tension with the ideas found in Job and Ecclesiastes. The writers of those books question why it is that bad things happen to good people if we are under God's wings of protection. Good people of faith in the Bible see this question from different perspectives. When I saw thousands of good people die along with terrorists who maliciously flew hijacked airplanes into buildings on September 11, 2001, I along with many others asked, "Why?" Where are the wings of protection? So it is still the unanswerable question. It is in the struggle, in the mystery of it, that we must dwell.

Let us pray:
Lord, help us understand what we can, and accept in faith what we cannot. Amen.

SUGGESTED PSALM: *Psalm 112*
SUGGESTED HYMNS:
  "Amazing Grace" (All)
  "Just As I Am" (B, C, E, F, P, UM)

Living by New Rules

Hearing the Word

The Beatitudes are the famous words that begin Jesus' Sermon on the Mount, which is found in Matthew chapters 5–7. The word blessed is sometimes translated as "happy." In the original language it is a rich word that is meant to convey both of these English words and more. Setting the tone for much of the Sermon on the Mount, Jesus begins with several surprising turnabouts. Happy (blessed) are the poor? Those who mourn? The meek? Those who are persecuted for doing what God requires? Some of those named are more expected: for example, happy are those who are merciful to others. The last two Beatitudes anticipate persecution and are drawn out in more detail than the others.

Living the Word

Team penning is an interesting and competitive event for people who enjoy riding horses and working with cattle. A team of riders, usually three, are turned loose in an arena with a small herd of cattle. Each cow has a number—say, from one to ten. The arena has a center line; the riders must not allow any cow to cross the line except the three they are assigned to pen. Further, those three have to cross the center line in order (for example, #6 first, then #7, then #8). Once on the other end, they must not cross back, in spite of their urge to run back and join the herd. Once all three are separated, in order, from the rest of the herd, then the team of riders must get all three to run inside a pen on their end of the arena, all the while preventing any of the rest of the herd from crossing the center line. It is a handful of work for three people on horses to do in less than ninety seconds. It would be one thing if the cattle would cooperate, but most of them seem to want to go the other way. The team with the fastest time wins, but in the process if even one cow steps across the line that should not, or is in the wrong order, the team is instantly disqualified. It is actually a wonder whenever a team can abide by the rules and get the job done at all.

Of course if the real point were just to get a certain three cows in the pen, and all the rules were not in the way, it would be a much easier job. In that case, the cowboys could simply know what they needed to accomplish, and do it in any way that works.

In a similar way, the Pharisees and other religious leaders of Jesus' day had twisted what it meant to be religious. They had created so many rules that they legislated the heart right out of it. Being a religious person had become an exercise in legalism; the Ten Commandments had been expanded into literally hundreds of detailed laws and regulations that only the most educated could hope to learn, let alone keep. As Jesus observed, the religious leaders had placed an impossible burden on the people with too many ways to be instantly disqualified. Jesus had a different, and more practical approach to religious faith. It was truly revolutionary for his day (and ours too). He made religion a matter of inward qualities, of character, and of relationship to God and neighbor.

Jesus' approach sorted through the rules to find the heart of the matter; instead of listening to a long list of rules about how to put three cows in a pen, he would have asked, "What is the point here: keeping one cow in a whole herd from making a wrong step, or getting the cows where you want them to go?" Jesus just had a special way of understanding and teaching others what it means to be truly religious.

There is still a lot of legalism floating around in today's religion. "Don't mow the grass on Sunday." "Don't sit on someone else's pew at church." (That's the unforgivable sin!) "Dress a certain way, talk a certain way, be a certain way." When religion amounts to a way to screen people out of our group, when it becomes an exercise in intolerance, then it is sinful and corrupted. Jesus saw that it boils down to loving God with all our heart, and loving our neighbor as we love ourselves. The Beatitudes could be seen as Jesus' Ten Commandments. They are not describing behavior and rules to keep, but inner qualities. That's the point of religion, at least the way Jesus saw it.

Let us pray:
Lord, help us see through the rules we put on ourselves to the grace and love that is your will for us to receive and put into practice. In Christ, Amen.

Counting on Resurrection

Hearing the Word

In 1 Corinthians 15, Paul's overarching theme is resurrection. One hint for his motivation about writing on this subject can be found in the question the people were asking, recorded in 15:12. The devotional text includes a brief creed (verses 3-5) that identifies the resurrection as a central tenet of the faith. The lesson text deals more directly with the implications of believing in the resurrection for Christians.

Whether Paul was really one of the apostles is questioned. He was not one of the Twelve, so the only way he met Jesus was in Paul's experience on the road to Damascus (after Jesus' death and resurrection). However, Paul argues that through God's grace, he has worked harder than the actual disciples. Therefore Christ's appearances after death extended not only to those who knew Jesus in life, but also to those such as Paul who did not.

Living the Word

Have you ever felt like you have ruined your life? Have you ever done something that seemed unforgivable? It can happen to anyone. Many people have a moment in their life, tucked away in the dimly lit corners of memory, that they would love to forget. It is a little like the pitcher who would like to have the baseball back after throwing the hanging curve in the bottom of the ninth inning in the final game of the World Series. But once the ball sails over the wall, it does not come back.

It is clear that Paul felt this way. He participated, with fervor, in the persecution of the church. He had stood by with approval while Stephen, the first Christian martyr, was stoned to death (see Acts 7:54–8:1). It must have been a gruesome and traumatic scene, one that was hard to forget. As the rocks whizzed through the air and thudded against Stephen's increasingly broken and bleeding body, surely his persecutors shouted insults and angry words. Yet he prayed for God to forgive his executioners. It was a horrible, bloody, violent murder of an innocent man, and Paul (called Saul at the time) stood on the wrong side.

For the rest of his life, Paul had to remember that violent act and live with regret. That is why it comes up in today's scripture as Paul talks about himself. He clearly felt guilt, regret, and sorrow for participating in that terrible, traumatic act that he could never undo. Some people in prison feel that way. They are forced to live for years with the consequences of an action and to be unable to change what they did. Even becoming a Christian in prison and being forgiven by God does not lessen their sentence, and sometimes Christians go to the death chamber with their regrets. The past can feel like a death sentence to any of us. One angry act can lead to guilt that can torture a person for the rest of his or her life.

In a sense, Paul "died" to his evil past, and was "resurrected" to a new person. In spite of being perhaps Christianity's single most important evangelist, he still experienced such regret about his past. But Paul didn't sentence himself to be spiritually dead the rest of his life, to let regret paralyze him. Instead, he not only received God's forgiveness but also rose up again and claimed a new and resurrected purpose in life. Had he tortured himself forever for what he had done, he could have been reduced to a person in deep spiritual pain, a person who was unable to go on with life.

One of the things I admire about Paul is that the Resurrection included him. Yes, his life was a little "abnormal" as he put it, but his rebirth was still real. When we claim the power of the Resurrection for our lives, it means that we can truly clean out all those dark corners of regret from the past, no matter how emotionally crippling they have been to us. New life in Jesus Christ means that God can give us a new purpose. Let the regrets go; claim God's new purpose for you and live it.

Let us pray:

Lord, thank you for the resurrection of Jesus; help us receive the hope and new beginning of resurrection in our own life too. Through Christ our risen, merciful, and loving Lord, Amen.

READ IN YOUR BIBLE: *2 Corinthians 4:16–5:5*   **November 21, 2004**
SUGGESTED PSALM: *Psalm 23*
SUGGESTED HYMNS:
  "Abide with Me" (B, C, E, F, L, P, UM)
  "There Is a Balm in Gilead" (B, E, F, P, UM, W)

New Beginnings

Hearing the Word

Paul was being criticized in Corinth; some scholars suggest that one of the criticisms leveled at him was that he could not really be an apostle since his body was obviously getting older and weaker. Of course that was a blatant misunderstanding of eternal life, and so Paul sought to correct the misunderstanding. He compares our mortal body to a tent, and our eternal life to a house in heaven. Paul makes good use of contrasts. The tent represents a temporary and transient existence (and remember that he was a tentmaker by trade). But a house is a permanent place built for the long term. In the same way, he labels the troubles we have with our physical bodies as temporary, and the glory that we will enjoy in heaven as eternal.

Living the Word

In February, when the Illinois ground was frozen solid, I took a ride on our two-year-old filly called Destiny. Her name nearly proved prophetic for me. Everything went well on our ride for about five minutes. Then a kitten ran in front, and you would have thought Destiny saw a ten-foot green monster. She did a couple of jumps, then tried to run while I tried to hold her back. Suddenly she went into a tizzy of bucking, and I knew that soon I would meet the ground. I hung on to the best of my ability for two tremendous bucks, but on the third we parted company. After a few moments in midair, I came back down, hard. I didn't even have time for my life to flash before my eyes.

At first I did not know the extent of my injuries, but I knew that I could not catch my breath. Fortunately, a friend rushed over and caught the wild-eyed horse. She said, "Just stay down. Just stay there." Soon I was able to breathe, but my whole rib cage was in

27

pain. I later learned that I broke ribs on both sides of my rib cage as well as separated ribs from my chest bone.

Eventually I got up, but for three or four weeks I could not lie down in a bed. I could only sleep if the back of the couch supported my ribs, and even that hurt. I am still fairly young, but suddenly I found I had a lot in common with some of the older folk in the congregation when they mentioned pains in their back or hip or shoulder. I listened with great interest to what they did to help endure the pain; suddenly the information was relevant to me.

It was also one more reminder that our life is temporary. In a flash, with the meow of a little kitten, or by failing to notice an oncoming car, or by being in the wrong place at the wrong time, our life can suddenly change, or even end. It is a difficult fact to face and truly absorb, but our body is temporary. (The message sinks in a little easier when you are popping pain medicine for broken ribs.) We often operate under the assumption that our body is something we will always have. But just as we will one day leave behind our possessions in this world, we will leave behind the body we live in.

Paul points out that our body is more like a tent than a house. Of course we should take care of it, but even people who jog ten miles a day and eat nothing but raw whole grain do not get to live in this old tent forever. As time goes by, we can see the signs of aging; a new wrinkle here, a gray hair (or missing hair!) there. It could be depressing to watch our body lose the fight with mortality, but happily God has something more permanent in mind for us—a house in heaven for our spirit.

Our bodies are God's way of providing a home for those of us who wander through the wilderness of this world; and they are good temporary homes. So don't spend too much time staring in the mirror or plucking the gray hairs out; our aches and pains are all temporary. There is no such thing as a permanent pain, and no such thing as a problem that will last forever. So be at peace, and focus on things that will last, such as the love and mercy of God, and the love we have for one another.

Let us pray:
Lord, thank you for your gifts to us, both those that are temporary and those that last forever. For you are faithful and good to us, both now and always. Help us trust you, be at peace, and have faith. Amen.

READ IN YOUR BIBLE: *Ephesians 2:4-10*   November 28, 2004
SUGGESTED PSALM: *Psalm 135*
SUGGESTED HYMNS:
  "O Come, O Come, Emmanuel" (B, E, F, L, P, UM, W)
  "O Come, All Ye Faithful" (All)

Becoming One Family

Hearing the Word

It would be difficult to find a more succinct and powerful brief explanation of the core of Christian theology than Ephesians 2:4-10. It clearly expresses the human condition, the spiritual death of sin. Then it offers an eloquent description of God's grace and what that means for us and for our salvation. Finally, it explains the relationship between our salvation and the ongoing work that we are called to do, not to build up merit but to fulfill God's righteous purpose for our lives. The lesson scripture immediately follows this devotional text. It deals with the salvation of the Gentiles, and one of the links between the two sections is that both Jews and Gentiles are saved by the grace of God and received into the family of God by God's gracious choice.

Living the Word

Out on the farm we have a small collection of barn cats. Some were someone else's that got transferred to our care and feeding; some just showed up out of nowhere and instead of visiting for a while, they moved in. Four are females. Not too long ago we had a fifth visitor—a romantic tomcat. That is how we had four sets of kittens within just a few days!

The first two litters were born the same morning. Each of the first-time mothers had four tiny kittens. One of them, Pester, still looked like she had more left to be born (we had heard that sometimes there can be a delay between babies). Sure enough, the next morning Pester had a total of six babies. However, we could not find all of the other mother's kittens. She only had two left, so we thought that overnight an animal might have gotten them. By that evening, Pester's litter had grown to seven kittens, and the other mother was down to one!

29

That was when we figured out that Pester was a catnapper. She was a new mother with kitten greed. To put a positive spin on it, her mothering instincts extended beyond her own kittens to the kittens of other mothers.

In the interest of justice, we redistributed the babies between the two young mothers, and moved their boxes right next to each other in a tiny "maternity ward" in the barn—two boxes, two mothers, and eight little kittens. The kittens were fortunate because even though they didn't know who their real mother was, they were all doubly blessed, since they all had a biological mother, but they also had another loving parent too.

In the same way that Pester went looking for additional kittens to love, God has first loved each of us—God has "adopted" us into the family. We have not done anything to earn it; it is just grace.

Once all the other kittens began to grow up, it was like a genuine cat herd in that barn. There were kittens everywhere, and mothers looking after them. Mothers would lie down and peaceably nurse their young, and all was well. It was a great environment for them to grow up, and they had all the love and attention they could want. Eventually they all went to good homes. We sponsored a trip to the vet for the mothers because we about ran out of friends who needed a cat.

It will be hard to forget what it was like in that barn for a while— all those kittens had all the love and nurture they could want, and there was joy and peace (well, at least when the kittens were asleep). It reminded me of the nativity scene in the Bible; at least it was in a barn, and the animals were there! But most of all, I think it was all those adopted kittens—it made me think of God's grace.

We have our biological family, but as Christians we also have been adopted as one of God's own. Like Paul wrote: "It is by God's grace that you have been saved through faith. It is not the result of your own efforts, but God's gift" (Ephesians 2:8-9).

Let us pray:
Lord, thank you for your love and grace. In this Christmas season, may we prepare ourselves for the birth of your Son, our Savior, Jesus Christ, who was born into the arms of a human mother and father, but who came to make us the children of God. Amen.

READ IN YOUR BIBLE: *Jeremiah 1:4-10*   **December 5, 2004**
SUGGESTED PSALM: *Psalm 99*
SUGGESTED HYMNS:
  "O Little Town of Bethlehem" (All)
  "Infant Holy, Infant Lowly" (B, F, L, P, UM, W)

The Call to Follow God

Hearing the Word

The similarity between today's devotion scripture and today's lesson scripture is rather obvious. Both are "call stories," which tell how Abram and Jeremiah first felt God's call in their life to do something special for God. Abram was already an old man when God called him in Genesis, while Jeremiah was "just a youth." Yet both of them seemed to be unlikely candidates because of their age. Most people would have thought that Abram was "too old" at the age of seventy-five to start out from home and begin an entirely new life. At the other end of the spectrum, Jeremiah felt he was too young to be God's spokesperson. In spite of any misgivings they may have had, God used each one in a major way.

Living the Word

Really, Jeremiah was probably right. He was still too young to be a prophet. If you think about it, that is a lot of responsibility for a young person. Imagine, after all, if you thought God wanted to enlist you! Imagine being responsible, like Jeremiah was, to write one of the top three biggest books by a prophet in the whole Old Testament. To write something that will be a top seller for centuries—that's pretty high expectations for just a youth, don't you think?

Not only that, but he also had to confront a whole country about the things they were doing wrong, and he had to be the major representative for an enormously influential and important client (God). Probably he needed a little more experience.

As a youth, you figure that to have the right amount of experience, you really ought to be at least thirty. The trouble is that by then most people are getting settled down in a new career, work-

31

ing extra hours to "get ahead," getting married, and maybe even having a child or two. Yes, it seems better to look more closely at forty years old. Also, as a result of successfully climbing the ladder at work, career responsibilities have really gotten out of hand. Come to think of it, forty is not a good time to serve God.

By age fifty to sixty-five, you are working extra hard to save up for retirement as well as pay off the kids' college loans. Graduations for the kids and weddings for them, and getting pictures of your grand-children, and taking care of aging parents, too—it is the "sandwich generation." There are far too many demands at that time to serve God. Can you imagine, on top of all of that, having to write a prophetic book, too? And none of that includes the time you'd have to spend running around confronting people about their sins. Do you know how mad that makes some people? You'd lose customers, and that would be bad for the business.

Maybe after retirement—that is when you are supposed to have time to do all the things you didn't have time to do before you retired. Most retirees say they have never been busier than after they retired. Maybe it is because everybody thinks that now retirees should have time to do all the things that people couldn't get them to do before retirement, like chair a committee at church.

After a decade or two of retirement, people have usually gotten the hang of it. They have their winter home down South paid off. The kids have scattered across the nation, and that means a lot of trips all over the place. But that's a great way to stay busy. You might get a little forgetful at that age too—go to the refrigerator but not remember what you wanted—but that's normal. Oh well. Then your preacher calls and asks if you will serve on a committee; they need somebody who will "get things going" down there at the church. Then you remember—that's what it was! You intended to serve God, but the time never was right before. So you think about it overnight and make up your mind: "No, I'd rather not," you say. "I'm too old. Get someone younger."

I don't know, but maybe that's how Jeremiah wound up with the job.

Let us pray:
Lord, help us find a way to serve you, not just at a certain age but at every age. Amen.

Leadership Qualities

Hearing the Word

Today's lesson scripture is about God's choice of David to be king of Israel (following King Saul, whom God had rejected). The devotional lesson takes place at a later time, after David is already king. In it he offers a prayer of thanksgiving to God for God's promise to bless David's descendants. David was a great and faithful king; during his reign Jewish history in the promised land in many ways reached its peak. After the kingdom was later divided, the Jewish people longed for another king like David, and it was thought that such a king would be a descendant of David's. That is why, during this Christmas season, Christians see a fulfillment of this promise to David in the birth of Jesus, the Messiah, who was in fact a descendant of King David (see the genealogies in Matthew 1:1-17 and Luke 3:23-38).

Living the Word

As they told me a few days later, a young boy at our church apparently told his parents, "I know what God's last name is!" Since they didn't know what God's last name is, nor had they probably ever thought about it, the parents were more than mildly curious. So they asked, "Well, what is it?"

He replied, "Rasche."

Of course they could hardly tell me about this because they were laughing so hard. But it was an honor that their son figured that God and I are related. His brother visited our old barn when we, along with his parents, were working on fixing it up. He asked what a certain structure was, and his father, who is a farmer, said rightly that it was an old wooden manger for feeding the animals that used to live in the barn. So ever since then that boy has been convinced that Jesus was born in our barn.

33

I suppose that these kinds of experiences are not too unusual for ministers. Not too many years ago, a young girl from another family thought that I was Jesus. Her mother read her children's storybooks about the Bible, and apparently she noticed that Jesus had a beard. Since I do too she insisted on calling me Jesus for months in spite of my and her mother's assurances that my name was really Jeff.

Children apparently wonder where God is, where Jesus is, and how all the biblical characters relate to us. To children, their world is right around them, and all the people they can imagine are pretty much just the people they know or see. So they are looking for God in the people they see right around them. Of course children leap to the wrong conclusion when they equate God with the preacher. The conclusion they *should* reach, and will see in time, is that God is to be found in *all* the people in the congregation.

The boy that thought God's last name was Rasche was a little confused but not far off the mark. He was wondering whose family God belongs to. Who is God's relative? This same thing mattered to the ancient Jewish people when they thought of the Messiah. It was important to them that the Messiah be one of King David's descendants because David was their greatest king. Both Matthew and Luke include a detailed family tree to demonstrate that Jesus was from the family of David. Luke takes it a step further and shows Jesus' lineage all the way back to Adam. He showed not only that Jesus was a fulfillment of their hope for a descendant of King David, but also that Jesus is a relative of us all.

Jesus criticized some of the Jewish people of his day who seemed to think that just because they were related to Abraham, they were "God's people," as though the only criterion is genealogy. No, he taught, what makes us true descendants is to live like we are part of God's family—to live up to the name.

So the question is not really what God's "last name" is. The question is this: no matter what your last name happens to be, does the name "Christian" fit you?

Let us pray:
Lord, thank you for sending your Son, who is also a relative of all of us, to be our Savior. Help us live up to your name, and act like we are all part of your family. Through Christ our Lord, Amen.

READ IN YOUR BIBLE: *Luke 1:26-32*   **December 19, 2004**

SUGGESTED PSALM: *Psalm 113*

SUGGESTED HYMNS:

  "It Came Upon a Midnight Clear" (All)

  "Angels We Have Heard on High" (B, E, F, L, P, UM, W)

When the Unexpected Happens

Hearing the Word

When today's devotional scripture from Luke is placed side by side with today's lesson scripture from Matthew, we see God at work with both Mary and Joseph to help prepare them for the unusual turn of events in their life. Typically, Jewish couples were first engaged to be married, perhaps as an arranged marriage from the time they were young. Later, they were betrothed, which was a more legal arrangement (more like our idea of engagement today). After a year of betrothal, the wedding itself occurred. Before the wedding, Joseph could have called off the marriage; in fact when he found out Mary was pregnant, he quietly planned to reject her.

The Davidic line of descent is traced through Joseph, even though Jesus was not technically Joseph's biological child. Yet these scriptures show that God intervened not only with Mary but also with Joseph. Both parents were people of great faith, a more important characteristic than mere biology.

Living the Word

Christmas unexpectedly sprung to life once again one Sunday evening at a Hanging of the Greens service. The children and youth of the church re-enacted the nativity story in words and song. Among the characters were angels and stars running hither and thither, a little feathered dove drinking from a sippy cup, children singing solos and reciting poetic lines, a beautiful little cow and

35

pig, wise men and shepherds in full costume, and a few adult workers who had definitely earned a "star in their crown."

Of course Mary and Joseph walked in at the appropriate time, cradling the Baby Jesus who was represented by a real baby, the first child of some members of the congregation.

The nativity story is simple and familiar. The baby is born, and then the wise men and shepherds come to worship him. Usually we leave the story there, in the manger, and don't think too much about what happened next. After the shepherds and wise men left, did they all "hit the hay"? Did they wander in to join the crowd in the hotel lobby watching the latest news on CNN?

That is why the next thing that happened the night of the Hanging of the Greens service grabbed my attention. As soon as the nativity scene was over, Jesus' mother, Mary, still in full costume, walked off the stage area and carefully handed the Baby Jesus, also still wrapped in swaddling clothes, to a woman in the crowd. Of course the woman was the baby's mother in real life. The savior of the world was simply handed over to a human being. And then it struck me: that is exactly what happened when God gave the care of the Baby Jesus to Mary and Joseph. *God placed the savior of the world into the hands of two human beings, Mary and Joseph.*

Have you ever heard about an owner of a company who began the company and has overseen its growth ever since? About such a person people sometimes comment, "That company is his or her 'baby.'" Sometimes it is difficult for such a leader to delegate authority to other people. Yet God has entrusted his plans, his "baby," into our care.

This Christmas, let us pause to think about God's children who have special needs, who are refugees of war, who are abused or neglected, who live below the poverty line, who are orphans, or who are sick. Some are children whose biological parents are addicted or abusive or negligent; some children run away from home, and others just feel isolated and alone right where they live.

Who will feed the hungry, wrap a blanket around the cold and homeless, and be a friend to those who feel alone? All these people are God's children, and they too have been entrusted into our care.

Let us pray:
Lord, as we look into the eyes of your precious Son in this season, may we receive him in our hearts, and be faithful in continuing your work in this world, especially with the children. In Jesus' name we pray, Amen.

READ IN YOUR BIBLE: *Psalm 71:1-8*   December 26, 2004

SUGGESTED PSALM: *Psalm 98*

SUGGESTED HYMNS:

  "Silent Night, Holy Night" (All)

  "We Three Kings" (B, E, F, P, UM, W)

Searching for Hope in the Right Places

Hearing the Word

Psalm 71:1-8 could easily be the words of Simeon or Anna, the two older adults who spent all their time at the temple, hoping for the Messiah, and whose dreams were fulfilled when they saw the Baby Jesus (recounted in the lesson scripture today). The occasion was the presentation of Jesus in the temple. According to Jewish law (see Exodus 13:2-13), the firstborn male child belonged to God, but a couple could go to the temple and "redeem" the child (buy the child back for a token offering), which was of course normative for couples to do. Even in the midst of the joy of Jesus' birth, however, Simeon sounds an ominous note of warning when he tells Mary that sorrow will break her heart. So Jesus' birth, life, and death are centered around the temple and events that take place there.

Living the Word

There is a term sometimes used by psychologists called "self-fulfilling prophecy." This means that if a person is given an expectation, the person tends to live up to (or down to) that expectation. If everyone in town expects a person to be a worthless drunk, that is how the person will likely behave. If everyone, on the other hand, expects that person to become a doctor or other professional person, then that person has a far better chance of it. It is just a tendency; not an iron-clad rule, but our expectations have great power in shaping the reality we eventually experience.

In the basketball movie "Hoosiers," the season benchwarmer

37

has to go in near the end of a key game in the state tournament. He is shorter and less skilled than the other players, and he knows it. When one of the stars fouled out, he did not even want to go on the floor, but the coach forced him. When his team was down by one point, the other team fouled him. In the huddle that followed, the coach (played by Gene Hackman), said to the players, "Now, *when* he makes his second shot"—then turning to the little guy, he said, "and you *will* make both shots"—"we need to get back on defense right away." Though his earlier shot had not come close to the basket, he had high expectations to live up to. If you want to know whether he made the shots, you must rent the video.

Simeon and Anna are a little like that coach. They expect great things for the Baby Jesus and say so. Imagine the impact that must have had on Jesus' parents. When they looked at Jesus as a toddler learning to walk, could they have known that someday he would walk on water. When he ate with them at their table, could they have expected him to feed the multitude with just a little bit of food. Doubtful they knew what to expect, but they did raise him knowing that he was a very special child, chosen by God to do great things.

The psalm that is today's devotional scripture (71:1-8) includes these words: "Sovereign Lord, I put my hope in you; I have trusted in you since I was young. I have relied on you all my life. . . . I will always praise you."

The world is hard enough to face, as it was for Jesus, without having to overcome a negative self-image. One thing children need at an early age is to be taught faith in God, and a positive outlook on their own future. Instead of telling children how they have been bad, catch them being good and really praise them for that. Tell the children in your life how much that is just like who you have always known them to be. Teach them to have faith in God to always be there for them in the future, and that God is determined to bless them.

Let us pray:
Lord, as we celebrate the birth of Jesus and the hope that his birth brought to the world, help us also give the gifts of a strong faith, a strong sense of hope, and good expectations for the future to the children we know and love, too. Through Christ, who was blessed with good parents and the love of a good faith community, Amen.

SUGGESTED PSALM: *Psalm 122*
SUGGESTED HYMNS:
  "More Love to Thee" (B, C, F, P, UM)
  "There Is a Wideness in God's Mercy" (All)

Spreading the Good News

Hearing the Word

The first portion of today's devotional and lesson scriptures, found near the beginning of Matthew and Mark, are almost identical. They tell the familiar story of how Jesus saw four fishermen (two at a time), called them to be his disciples, and how they left their nets to follow him. With that, Jesus immediately gets down to the business of teaching, preaching, and healing the sick in Matthew's Gospel. Instead of more summary, Mark focuses on the healing of one man who has an evil spirit. Shortly before the evil spirit is cast out, it identifies Jesus as the Messiah only twenty-four verses into Mark's Gospel. Mark also offers a summary of the beginning of Jesus' work. Both Gospel writers agree that it got off to a great start. The word about Jesus spread rapidly, and many people flocked to him and were healed.

Living the Word

As we begin a new year, half a decade into the new millennium already, maybe it is a good time to look back at the past five years since the 2000 celebration. Is your church growing, reaching more people, engaged in more missions, and making a bigger impact in your community than it was five years ago? Or, is the opposite true?

It is impressive that Jesus had not even gotten all twelve disciples together yet, but was already engaged in an active and growing ministry. The word of his ministry spread fast, and people flocked to see him. In many churches we worry about trying to keep the dwindling number of members we have; and other churches do grow rapidly. What is the difference?

At the core is whether or not people really want to come to your church, and that largely depends on what you offer them. Jesus

39

was wildly popular, at least at first, because he could heal people, and there are a lot of sick people who want to be healed. His ministry grew rapidly because he knew, and met, the needs of people.

One cartoon shows an architect showing a church committee his model of a new church building shaped like a football stadium. He says, "This model is designed to increase the number of men in your church." So, short of building stadiums, what is it that will help us grow instead of shrink?

This scripture suggests that we are "in business," first of all, to know the needs of the people around us, like Jesus did. The church is often guilty of talking more than we listen. The best ministry begins by really listening, by asking questions, by learning more about our communities and the needs of the individuals in them. Too often we "take our message to the people" without listening first; it is like the game show in which you speak an answer and then try to guess the question. It's a little backward, isn't it?

Second, the fishermen did not come into the temple, tug Jesus' cloak, and ask if they could sign up. He went to where they were and invited them to follow. Too often we look around at church to see who is there instead of going out into the world to see who might come there. Simple invitations work wonders.

Third, we need to try new things, like Jesus did. He did not just follow the pattern of preachers of his day. He was new and different. Suppose every year your church has had seven hundred people at an annual meal, but only twelve at a Bible study? Maybe it is time to find some creative ways to bring the Bible to the dinner.

Fourth, and most important, we must focus on the good news of Jesus Christ. That is our difference from clubs, schools, or sports. Take a hard look at the "messages" your church gives out, from your outdoor signs to the words used in worship to welcome guests. I have been in church and listened to whole sermons that criticize.

As long as the church offers good news for the lost, the hungry, the lonely, and the sick, we will continue to be a viable and effective witness for Jesus in this millennium and the next.

Let us pray:
Lord, as we pass from one year into the next we pray that we may follow your leading. Be our guide into the future, and teach us to reach out to others with the love and kindness you showed in your life. Amen.

"Lord, Speak to Me" (B, C, F, L, P, UM)
"Come, We That Love the Lord" (B, C, E, F, UM, W)

Sharing God's Hospitality

Hearing the Word

To understand today's devotional lesson, it is important to read the few verses that precede it. In this portion of Ephesians, Paul is talking about getting rid of the "old self," and putting on the "new self." That is why he paints a contrast between things that would be typical of the old self and things that are part of the new self. For example, consider the contrast between robbing and earning an honest living so as to be able to help the poor. Even for people who have not been robbers, such specific examples indicate that Paul expects the Christian's life, values, and actions to change.

Living the Word

One day a man saw an old friend in a store. After greeting him, he asked, "And how is your wife?"
The friend replied sullenly, "She's in heaven now."
With that the surprised man recoiled in shock and embarrassment. All he could manage to say was, "Oh! That's *horrible!*"
Of course saying it was horrible for her to be in heaven did not seem like the right thing to say. So he corrected himself, "What I mean is, that's *great!*"
That didn't seem exactly right, either; so he attempted to recover by adding, "What I really mean to say is, I'm *surprised!*"
Sometimes it is difficult to find just the right word, isn't it? One of the changes that Paul thought that being a Christian should make is in always using the right kinds of words. He felt that they should refrain from harmful words, and instead use only the kind that build people up.
This change is more difficult than it would seem. James aptly comments,

41

> All of us often make mistakes. But if a person never makes a mistake in what he says, he is perfect and is also able to control his whole being. We put a bit into the mouth of a horse to make it obey us, and we are able to make it go where we want.... We humans are able to tame and have tamed all other creatures—wild animals and birds, reptiles and fish. But no one has ever been able to tame the tongue.... We use it to give thanks to our Lord and Father and also to curse other people, who are created in the likeness of God. Words of thanksgiving and cursing pour out from the same mouth.... [T]his should not happen! (James 3:2-3, 7-10)

But it does happen. One of the most difficult things for the Lord to convert is what we speak. Somehow we carry the old rhyme in our being: "Sticks and stones may break my bones, but words will never hurt me." So we often fail to fully appreciate the impact of our words; it is *not* true that they do not hurt others. In fact, they often hurt *worse* than sticks or stones.

I once did a funeral for a schoolteacher whose student commented that she was the only teacher that never said a cross word to him, and he freely admitted that he had been a challenge to all of his teachers. Several adults commented, in all sincerity, that they had never heard her utter a word of criticism about another human being. That did not mean that she was a pushover. She was willing to disagree tactfully, but she did so without belittling another person who held a different view. Further, she often had kind, uplifting, and complimentary things to say to people. When they were out of her presence, she did not turn on them and gossip about them, either. In short, when it came to words she had evidently gone a long way in putting off the old self and putting on the new self.

Conversion of our words is as difficult as getting the poison out of a polluted river, but not impossible. Like all aspects of our salvation, what is impossible for a human being is possible with God.

Let us pray:
May the words of my mouth and the thoughts of my heart be acceptable to you, O Lord, my strength and my redeemer. Amen.

READ IN YOUR BIBLE: *Luke 9:1-6*

SUGGESTED PSALM: *Psalm 37:1-11*

SUGGESTED HYMNS:

"Have Thine Own Way, Lord" (B, C, F, UM)

"Holy, Holy, Holy" (All)

Preparing for the Job

Hearing the Word

Today the devotional scripture and lesson scripture are parallel passages. The Synoptic Gospels (Matthew, Mark, and Luke) contain numerous sections that overlap one another. It is clear that in some order, one or two copied sections fairly directly, with few modifications, from the others. (Most scholars think that Mark was written first, and then Matthew and Luke created their Gospels using Mark and a "lost gospel" called "Q" as their source. But a minority believe Matthew and Luke were written first, and then Mark was written to include the material they shared in common.) This is not plagiarism. Instead, each Gospel writer chose to include or exclude certain events, both previously written and from their own knowledge, that helped them meet their own unique purposes. All three Synoptic Gospel writers included the sending out of the twelve disciples, so that was a key event for all of them.

Living the Word

Once I "shook the dust" off my feet in a mall. It was really a surprisingly satisfying experience. My wife is a freelance commercial artist. Most companies are appreciative of her work and treat her fairly, but, to make a long story short, one company was deceptive with her. They took advantage of her goodwill in the beginning stages of their working relationship, and suddenly numerous pieces of her artwork were applied to products that were not part of the original understanding—all without additional pay. So the first day she saw a display of her artwork on all those products in a store, she was upset. I didn't know what to say to make her feel better, so as we left the store I said "Wait a minute." I then took off my shoes and pretended to shake the dust off of them. She

43

laughed, and we went on our way. That company is still not in her good graces, but now they have done all the harm they can—it's over with and behind us.

I was thinking about Jesus' suggestions to the disciples about how to handle rejection when seeking to win disciples. He told them to "shake the dust" off their feet. These days we mostly walk on asphalt and concrete; and even when we are in a dusty place, our shoes generally protect our feet from the dust better than the sandals of olden days did. But in Jesus' day, a good host would offer his or her guests water to wash their feet after walking on the dirt roads. It was a sign of hospitality, of welcome, and of a friendly reception.

Naturally, when the disciples encountered a negative reaction, nobody offered them an opportunity to wash their feet. So shaking the dust off their feet would have been a way of saying, "This was a bad experience, but I'm going to put it behind me and carry on." It was good for a person's mental well-being to leave rejection and hurt behind and move on.

There are times in our life when we need to shake the dust off our feet. It is easy to let one bad relationship so consume us with anger that it dampens the happiness we should be having with other people. That is a good time to pause, shake the dust off, and then move ahead. Or maybe, after twenty years of devoted service to a company, you are suddenly forced into early retirement in some job-slashing move designed to give the stockholders an extra 5 percent gain this year. It is lousy treatment, to be sure, but what about the next twenty years of your career? It is time to pause, shake the dust off, and move on down the road to another job opportunity.

There are many situations in which anger and hurt are justified, and rejection is difficult for anyone to take. When Jesus sent the disciples out into the cold, cruel world, he told them not to take an extra shirt or extra food, and he did give them one little nugget of wisdom to carry with them: When you are hurt, angry, and rejected, take your shoes off, shake that dust off—really shake those sandals hard, and make sure there is not a speck left on them—then put the shoes back on, and keep walking. There's a better day ahead.

Let us pray:
Lord, be with those who are hurting today, or who still carry anger or resentment with them. Help all of us know when to shake the dust off our feet, that we may always have the joy in living and the hope for the future that you intend for us to have. Amen.

READ IN YOUR BIBLE: *Matthew 16:24-28*   **January 23, 2005**

SUGGESTED PSALM: *Psalm 95:1-7*

SUGGESTED HYMNS:

"*Take Up Thy Cross*" (B, E, L, P, UM, W)

"*O Master, Let Me Walk with Thee*" (B, C, E, F, L, P, UM)

Giving Your All

Hearing the Word

One of the pivotal moments in Jesus' life was the first time he spoke about his own death to his disciples. Peter had just finished giving the correct answer to the big question, "Who do you say I am?" by replying that Jesus is "the Messiah, the Son of the living God" (Matthew 16:15). Then as soon as Jesus began to talk about his own death, Peter rebuked Jesus for talking that way; he was not prepared for such a thought. And for that, Jesus rebuked Peter. Today's devotional scripture is Jesus' follow-up explanation as he explained how difficult it would be for the disciples to follow Jesus. He would tell them what it meant to be a disciple.

Living the Word

One of the great programs some schools have is to send home, overnight, Baby Think It Over®. The baby is a lifelike computerized doll. It cries, coos, burps, and even—yes, it sometimes needs new diapers. The young teen given charge of the baby wears a wristband with a metal "key" for the baby, so that only that youth can render the care the baby needs.

The computer inside the baby records how long it takes the young caretaker to respond to whatever the baby needs once it starts crying. At night the baby cries demand attention just like a real baby. So far two of my sons, as part of their classes, have been required to take the baby home overnight. I can't say that for them to know it is to love it. It was such a burden that they went to school early just to turn it in as soon as possible. One of my sons had it for a weekend, which meant three *long* nights. After waking up several times on both Friday and Saturday nights, he went to

45

bed early Sunday. He barely had time to fall asleep when we could hear the baby start to cry. My son was so zonked we had to go wake him up so he could take care of the baby. After being fed and having its diaper changed, the baby kept crying. All my son could think of was to burp it, but after forty-five minutes of patting its back it still had not burped. Finally, after rocking the baby for a while it went to sleep, and there was peace in the house—temporarily!

Baby Think It Over® helps young teens realize how much work is involved in taking care of a baby. If it were a theological baby and could talk, it might ask the youth, "Are you ready to take up your cross, forget yourself, and dedicate your life to me?"

Most teens figure out that, after taking care of Baby Think It Over®, for them the answer is "No, I am not ready to forget myself just yet." After all, you can't negotiate with a baby ("Let's sleep another five hours and then I'll give you chocolate milk instead of that old yucky formula. How would that be?"). No, the baby makes a demand, and the parent must forget his or her own needs and put the baby first. That is what it takes to be a mature adult who is responsible for a baby.

In much the same way, when Jesus spoke to the disciples about his own death, he told them that in order to follow him they would need to forget themselves. In a sense, Jesus is the Baby Think It Over® who grew up and now can talk, who asks us, "Are you ready to forget yourself and follow in my footsteps?" To do so means to put others first instead of our own plans and wishes. It is taking up our own cross because sometimes our fondest dreams and ideals have to die, to take a back seat to what God wants us to do.

No, it is not easy. The disciples tried to follow Jesus, but even they ended up scattering when the going got really tough. So who can really do this? Who can truly forget himself or herself and focus only on Christ and his will? Maybe no human can on our own; but with God anything is possible.

Let us pray:

Lord, help me learn to put your will first in my life, the needs of others second, and my will third. Help me forget myself, or at least that part of me that is not in keeping with your perfect will, that I may follow you and serve others in your name. Amen.

SUGGESTED PSALM: *Psalm 93*

SUGGESTED HYMNS:

"*Onward Christian Soldiers*" *(B, C, E, F, L, UM)*

"*Praise to the Lord, the Almighty*" *(B, E, F, L, P, UM, W)*

Moving Toward Greatness

Hearing the Word

Today's devotional reading is similar to the last part of the lesson scripture. One difference is that in Matthew's Gospel, the mother of James and John makes the request of Jesus on behalf of her sons; but in Mark's Gospel the two sons make the request directly. The point of the incident is the same: these two disciples wanted to receive glory, honor, and recognition. But Jesus pointed out that their real goal should be to serve others instead of seeking recognition. The fact that the other disciples were angry helps show why this principle is important. When people love one another, they think of the other person first; this has a tendency to strengthen a relationship. But when people love themselves more than others, it hurts relationships.

Living the Word

One day a boy found a purse sitting by a park bench. He found the name and phone number of the owner and gave her a call. When he returned the purse to her, she opened her billfold. "Hey!" she exclaimed. "I thought I had a one-hundred-dollar bill in here! Now there are five twenties!"

With that the boy confessed. "I did that, Ma'am," he said, "The last time I found a lady's purse she didn't give me a reward because all she had in her purse were big bills."

That boy was interested in service, but he was also interested in his reward. He is not so different from most of us. One of the ongoing conversations between some parents and their children goes something like this:

PARENT: I need you to mow the grass today.

47

CHILD: Am I going to get paid?

PARENT: No! It is just a chore; we all have chores to do.

CHILD: But Jimmy's parents pay him to mow their grass—he gets $20 every time he does it!

PARENT: Yep, I guess you got stuck with the wrong set of parents! We are all part of this family, and we all have our jobs to do. Now please get mowing!

Before we rush to blame the child for being greedy, we need to remember that we live in an economy that is built upon the principle that people are rewarded for their productivity, and that is the main factor that drives them to increased productivity. In other words, if you didn't get paid for your work, would you still do it?

This same attitude spills over into our religion. Even in that we want to receive a reward. In fact, the reward of heaven is one central idea of our faith. Asking "Would you still want to be a Chris-tian even if you thought there was no such thing as heaven?" is much like asking "Would you continue doing your job if there was no pay?" So, it is not particularly noble or pretty, but like rats in a laboratory experiment, we are motivated by future rewards and punishments.

Serving one another only "for pay" (as a way to get ourselves into heaven) is not the attitude Jesus wants us to cultivate. Otherwise his saying "the last will be first, and the first will be last" could be taken as instructions about how to get to the head of the line. The method is just to grab the least important seat and wait patiently—and then voila! You get to sit in the place of honor! (It's a good thing Jesus taught us how to get ahead of the rest of the crowd in heaven.)

James and John's request for a place of honor is just a little grandiose icing on the cake we all eat of "looking out for number one." So please don't judge them too harshly; they are too much like the rest of us. Jesus is trying to teach them, and us, that religion for a reward is still just another form of selfishness. If you want to emulate the disciples, then this is not their best moment to imitate. Is it okay with you to make others number 1, and let yourself be number 2?

Let us pray:

Lord, help us as we wrestle with our selfish nature, which even finds its way into our faith. Teach us what it means to forget ourselves and follow you completely, that we may do your will without asking what is in it for us. Through Christ, who put us sinners first, Amen.

"*Savior, Like a Shepherd Lead Us*" *(B, C, E, F, L, P, UM)*
"*My Shepherd Will Supply My Need*" *(B, E, F, P, W)*

Overcoming Grief

Hearing the Word

Psalm 31:9-15 captures at least two feelings of a grieving person that often go hand in hand. The first is, of course, deep sorrow and emotional pain. The second is the feeling of abandonment by friends. Psalm 31:5 contains the last words of Jesus from the cross (and also the last words of Stephen as he was stoned to death). At that time, Jesus felt both the pain and suffering of a man about to die, and also the pain caused by the abandonment of his friends. Today's lesson scripture is from the beginning of Ruth; again it is a scene of grief, but Ruth, instead of going back to "her own people," elected to stay with Naomi. It is a sign that she did not want to feel abandoned, cut off from the family she had left.

Living the Word

We have a cat named "Baby." She had one litter of kittens before "the trip" to the vet. We found good homes for all of her kittens, but she was a devoted mother. Soon after the last kitten went to live with someone else, we heard a strange, guttural yowling in the next room. It sounded like a deep cry, and is the most forlorn sound that I believe a cat can make. We peeked around the corner, and Baby was walking around carrying a Davy Crockett-style hat (a fur hat with an animal tail on the back). She must have found it in a closet, but it looked a lot like the color of her kittens. She carried that hat around for about thirty minutes, all the while yowling pathetically.

The next night, we heard the yowling again, and sure enough she was carrying around that hat. Although two years have passed, this has become a nightly routine. It is sometimes difficult to understand what a cat is thinking (they have tiny brains), but it appears that she has never stopped missing her kittens.

Of course if you know any person who has lost a loved one, then you know that grief lasts a long time. They usually reach a point, in time, of acceptance, though that is typically after a long and difficult patchwork of feelings that often include denial, shock, anger, guilt, depression, and just plain sorrow. Still, even the stage of acceptance does not mean that the loss has not made a life-changing mark. It is like topping a mighty old oak tree. Once you cut off all those great old branches that reach the sky, new sprouts may grow and form a new leafy top, but it is never the same as it was.

This psalm captures one of the most difficult aspects of grief, and that is the feeling of abandonment by friends. Of course friends usually rally around before and during a funeral, and sometimes they stop by afterward, too. But the peak needs for a grieving person are often in the long weeks and months after the funeral—right when everyone else has "gotten back to normal." If such a hurting person attempts to open up about his or her pain to friends, it is common for those friends to try to make him or her feel better. This is a useless tactic, and one that simply underscores the deep divide that exists between a person who fails to understand the reality of grief, and a person who feels depressed or alone in their grief. Or, if the friend really does listen carefully to all that pain, it is difficult for him or her to shoulder it over and over again for months or even years.

In every church and community there are many people who have lost a loved one in the past one to three years. One of the greatest ministries that all of us, lay or clergy, can do is to understand the long-term nature of grief, to listen far more than we talk, to refrain from trying to say trite or theological things that are designed to make it okay or make the person feel better. Instead, a true friend is one that is willing to "walk through the valley of the shadow of death," and not to try to change the valley into something it is not.

Let us pray:
Lord, thank you for being there for all of us in every joy or sorrow. Please be with those who grieve today. Open my eyes to their needs, and open my ears to listen, that those persons may never feel alone. Through Christ, Amen.

SUGGESTED PSALM: *Psalm 94:1-15*

SUGGESTED HYMNS:

"*Lord, I Want to Be a Christian*" (B, C, F, P, UM)

"*Holy God, We Praise Thy Name*" (E, F, L, P, UM, W)

Overcoming Pride

Hearing the Word

Today's devotional scripture is linked to the lesson scripture by the question of what makes a person clean or unclean; and pride such as Naaman first showed in the lesson scripture is one example of what Jesus said makes a person unclean. A reading of Leviticus, for example, shows that the Jewish laws paid close attention to things that created the condition of being unclean (such as touching a dead body), and the steps required to become clean again. Some of these laws would have had practical benefits (such as hand washing before eating, or eliminating household molds). However, Jesus' point was that genuine religion is far more than obeying a complex set of external laws; it is an inward matter of the heart.

Living the Word

The story goes that one day a high-ranking military officer noticed a lowly private walking toward his office. Determined to show his power and authority, the officer grabbed his telephone and began snapping orders into it just as the private entered. "Now get everything ready for our arrival at 0800 hours sharp at our usual meeting place—have the red carpet and the band ready to greet the president and myself before our meeting that morning. Now get on it!"

With that, he slapped the phone down, looked at the private, and barked, "And what do you need, private?"

"Oh, nothing," the private quietly replied. "I was just sent to repair your phone."

Pride was one of the things on Jesus' list that makes a person spiritually unclean. What did he mean by that?

There is something inside us that wants to impress other people.

51

We call it pride. Maybe this is a leftover trait from our "animal nature." After all, there are many animals that compete for the attention of a mate. For example, some birds must put on the most impressive display or build the most attractive nest to win a mate. Wolves must fight between themselves to be top dog in the pack. So perhaps pride is just a sign that we are still influenced by our animal nature. We want to be thought of as the top dog, and in the business world it is not unlike the law of the reef—eat others or be eaten. At least in the animal world pride has a legitimate function. For humans, though, pride can be a destructive force. We have the capacity to overcome it, especially with God's help.

I like the story of the retired minister who was a guest speaker at a church. He was trying to be humble when he told the congregation that a guest speaker is not like their own minister—he compared being a guest speaker to a temporary plastic covering over a window instead of the real panes of glass. On the way out near the end of the line a woman came through, intending to pay him a compliment. "Oh, Reverend, you were far more than just a cheap temporary cover over the window! You were a *real pane*!" See? God can help us overcome pride!

Not all pride is bad. Many people take pride in their work. For example, an artist might feel proud of a particular painting, a child might feel proud of a modeling clay sculpture. Pride crosses the line, though, when it changes from a positive self-evaluation to a comparison with others in order to put them down. When we think, like the officer at the beginning of this devotional article, "I'm better than that person," then that becomes sinful pride. This is an important distinction, because in the name of Christianity the positive kind of pride has gotten a bad name along with sinful pride, leading many to think that to be Christian they need to put themselves down, deny all legitimate compliments, and have low self-esteem. Yet there is a difference between being self-sacrificial and being self-deprecating. God didn't intend for us to have a miserable self-image—after all, he made us in the image of God!

Let us pray:
Lord, save me from comparing myself pridefully to others; instead, help me rejoice with others in their strengths, and come to an honest and realistic appreciation of the gifts you have given me, too. Amen.

SUGGESTED PSALM: *Psalm 34:1-8*

SUGGESTED HYMNS:

"*Amazing Grace*" *(All)*

"*Jesus, Lover of My Soul*" *(B, C, E, F, P, UM)*

Overcoming Uncertainty

Hearing the Word

Taken together, the devotional reading and the lesson reading for today make up the story of Jesus and Nicodemus, as well as Jesus' theological reflections at the end of their visit. Nicodemus was a Pharisee. The Pharisees were among Jesus' harshest critics, so he did not want his visiting with Jesus to be seen by his peers. Therefore he came to see Jesus at night, presumably when Jesus would have retreated to the countryside for the evening. In John's Gospel, light and darkness, day and night are symbolic for belief or unbelief, faith in God or rejection of God. So it is also symbolic that John pointed out that the visit occurred at night.

Living the Word

I'm just wondering how our world might be different if, instead of coming into the world to be our Savior, Jesus had said to Nicodemus in John 3:17, "For God did not send his Son into the world to be its savior, but to be its judge."

I can imagine a car wreck at a city intersection. The police rush to the scene. A woman is injured behind the wheel, and her child in the backseat is cut and bleeding. The policeman bends to look inside the car, pulls out a ticket, and says, "First of all, Ma'am, I can see you aren't wearing your seatbelt. That's the first ticket I can give you. Second, your child was not properly fastened in a child restraint seat." Then he turns to another officer at the scene. "Have you figured out whose fault it was yet?"

"Yep," answers the other officer. "It was hers. She ran a red light, and witnesses said she was speeding. So that will be two more tickets, plus you could give her another one for reckless driving ... and hey, another one for malicious endangerment."

53

Continuing this line of thought in a different incident, a lifeguard sees a fishing boat overturn far from shore. He plunges in and swims vigorously up to the fishermen. Pausing, he scolds, "You should have been wearing your life preservers!" Then he turns around and swims back to shore.

Yes, if Jesus came to be our judge and not our savior, then he would have come to earth to catch us in a mistake. He would have been far better at exposing our sins than any investigative reporter. And like investigative reporters do, as soon as he had some dirt on us from our past, he could have let everyone know so that we would be thoroughly shamed in public. He could have discredited us, tarnished our credentials, and ruined our reputations. And it would have all been the simple truth—just a little honest criticism from a God that sees what is wrong with every single detail of our thoughts, our actions, our attitudes, and even the things we leave undone that we should have done. But you know, if we can't live with that kind of honesty, then what's the matter with us anyway?

Instead of coming to bring good news for the poor, as he quoted as his mission statement from Isaiah 61:1-3, he would have come to get after the poor for dragging everyone else down—you know, tell them to quit being so lazy and get to work if they want to eat! Poverty must be their fault in some way, right?

If Jesus came to judge us instead of save us, he could have told us all the mistakes we ever made, and why all those choices were so unhealthy and unchristian and wrong. People would have flocked to him, and one at a time he could have given them a healthy dose of criticism. But for some reason when old Nicodemus came sneaking out there at night to see Jesus, hiding from his Pharisee peers, Jesus forgot to say "Shame on all of you Pharisees for plotting to kill me!" Instead, he said that he came into the world to be—let's make sure to get it right this time—our savior, and not to be our judge. *What a difference that makes!*

Let us pray:
Lord, thank you for seeking to save us from our sins, and not just to criticize us or shame us for our sins. Forgive us for being so fast to judge others; help us seek to offer help and compassion and love instead of criticism. In your mercy we pray, Amen.

READ IN YOUR BIBLE: *John 4:35-42*   **February 27, 2005**
SUGGESTED PSALM: *Psalm 134*
SUGGESTED HYMNS:
  "*Guide Me, O Thou Great Jehovah*" *(B, C, E, F, P, UM)*
  "*How Firm a Foundation*" *(All)*

Overcoming Prejudice

Hearing the Word

In the devotional portion of this scripture, Jesus quotes a contemporary proverb: "Four more months and then the harvest" (John 4:35). But Jesus points out that the "harvest" is already here and now. That is, there are those who are ready to believe in Christ right now, and others for whom all we can do is plant the message. For this Samaritan woman, you could say that the message was planted within her, and the same day she was "ready for harvest." She then became a sower right away. Some of the people she told believed on the basis of her testimony, and others only believed after they had seen Jesus for themselves. This may help explain what Jesus meant in verses 37 and 38. The disciples are not the only workers in the field; they may benefit from the work of others, or others may reap the benefits of their work.

Living the Word

One of the issues clergy face is whether to go back to previous churches to help with weddings, funerals, or other special events.

There are at least two schools of thought among clergy about whether to go back. Probably the majority view is that clergy should not go back in a pastoral capacity. There are several reasons. First, the most important one is that clergy are all working together and should respect one another's abilities to perform services for the people they are sent to serve at the time. Thus, if the bride does not know the current minister, then the wedding is a good way for her to come to appreciate that minister's gifts and graces, too. Like Jesus said, one person plants, another one reaps the harvest.

A second reason is that if clergy regularly did this, then the longer their past was, the more they would have to leave their current appointment to go to other places—and these can be scattered widely geographically, making any trip time consuming. Eventually clergy have to draw the line just out of sheer time constraints.

Third, once the service is over, the previous pastor returns to his or her new home and is not available for follow-up care, while the person who does live in town now to give that care is not the person who did the service. All of these reasons tend to discourage pastors from going back.

Now for an argument on the other side: it is true that people sometimes do form special relationships with a certain pastor, and why should they be denied the joy of sharing a wedding or the opportunity to support each other in a time of grief? After all, can't a parishioner love more than one pastor, and appreciate each of them for their own gifts and abilities? Therefore the other school of thought takes a more moderate view, like "Maybe on some rare occasions I will make an exception and assist, as long as the host pastor invites me to come."

This is not an issue easily solved if you have a heart for the people's wishes as well as an understanding of the good reasons for professional boundaries between pastors. This is one area where Jesus' words seem relevant. Our task is not to compete for the love of the people or to try to see every task through "on our watch." Rather, we are coworkers in God's field. To the extent that anyone goes back, it is important for both pastors (and people) to remember that some sow, some reap, but all are working for the same harvest together.

This can also apply to laypersons who take over teaching a class or chairing a committee or leading the youth group after other beloved leaders have moved on. The more we can respect the work of everyone, those who come before and those who come after, and affirm our different gifts, the better. It is all God's harvest, and we are coworkers in the field.

Let us pray:
Lord, help us respect the work and role of those who come before us and those who come after us, remembering that we are all part of your work. Help us see and affirm the good gifts in each leader or each group of people we work with. Through Christ, who is there at the planting and the harvest, Amen.

READ IN YOUR BIBLE: *Psalm 59:1-5*   **March 6, 2005**

SUGGESTED PSALM: *Psalm 14*

SUGGESTED HYMNS:

   "Abide with Me" (B, C, E, F, L, P, UM)

   "There Is a Balm in Gilead" (B, E, F, P, UM, W)

None Is Righteous

Hearing the Word

Some of the psalm writers make no secret about how they feel about their enemies, and this verse is from one of those psalms: "Wake up and punish the heathen; show no mercy to evil traitors!" (Psalm 59:5). The psalms include the full range of human emotion. The psalmist sounds like a person who has enemies plotting to kill him; in this way it reminds us of Jesus at this Lenten time of year. The lesson scripture from Romans includes quotations from other psalms that are similar to this one; the difference is that all of us are defined as sinners, and the psalm is used to describe sinners.

Living the Word

In 2003 the headlines announced the killing of Saddam Hussein's two sons Uday and Qusay in a firefight with U.S. soldiers. At about the same time Bob Hope died at the age of one hundred. When Bob Hope died, there was an outpouring of emotion around the world; he was remembered for all of the good things he had done. By contrast, there were not many tears shed, at least not by those who appeared on our American TV, for the sons of Saddam Hussein. The stories of how his sons tortured people, raped women, and murdered people on a whim were horrifying. The sons were the enemies of many people, including, at least in their final years of life, America as a country.

Meanwhile, at the time of this writing, Saddam himself remained still on the loose, and many months after September 11, 2001, Osama bin Laden had not been caught. For good reason our nation labeled these people, and the leaders under them, as our enemies. It is no secret that our leadership and military wanted them dead.

Seeing Uday and Qusay's battered bodies in the magazine pictures did not bring any grief to me, but it did not bring any joy either. I didn't dance in the street; I just felt like I was seeing the tragic (and predictable) end of a horrific story. Judging from what I had read, they lived a life of terrorizing, raping, torturing, and murdering their own people. For Saddam to issue a taped statement calling them "martyrs" seemed so twisted and distorted that it defied explanation.

So when the psalms speak passionately about evil men, asking God to destroy them, it seems understandable on some level to us today. After all, we wanted our enemies dead, and the world is certainly a bit safer, at least for some people, when these particular enemies have been captured or killed.

On the other hand, the killing of Uday and Qusay seemed like a hollow "victory." From a Christian standpoint, I think it is because they were not "redeemed." Merely killing them did not change them. They are just dead physically, but their spirit was never won over. That is why it seemed like a tragic waste of life not only in what they did to so many of their own citizens and our soldiers, but also in what happened to them.

All of this makes the Christian message all the more powerful. As disgusting as we find our "enemies" to be, it comes as a shock to be labeled as the enemy of God ourselves (see Romans 3:9-20 and 5:1-12). It is a further shock to discover that God's response to us as sinful enemies is not to simply kill us. Instead, God wants to redeem us, to change us into friends. Therefore this is not a waste of life; it is a miracle of grace—a quite different ending to the story!

The week that Uday and Qusay died, the magazines and television networks showed the world photos of what it means to give enemies the treatment they deserve. That is justice. It is difficult for the message to sink in deeply enough for us to see how fortunate we are to have a God who goes beyond justice to mercy and grace. For we were once enemies, but through Christ, God has changed us from enemies into God's friends.

Let us pray:
Lord, thank you for your grace and mercy, which is more than we can ever comprehend. Forgive us of our sins, change our ways, and help us live up to the status of friend you have granted to us. Through Christ our Lord and Redeemer, Amen.

SUGGESTED PSALM: *Psalm 50:16-23*

SUGGESTED HYMNS:

  "Just As I Am, Without One Plea" (B, C, E, F, L, P, UM)
  "There's a Wideness in God's Mercy" (All)

God Judges All People

Hearing the Word

Even though nobody really thought that God would appear in a courtroom and bring a case against Israel, the poetic imagery used in this psalm is a powerful tool that is used in other places in the Bible. For example, see Job 13 in which Job brings a case against God. Another example can be found in Micah 6:1-5. God's main "complaint" is that the people are confining their faith to the giving of sacrifices, but God wants them to feel and to be thankful—not just trudge in and throw a sacrificed animal on the altar.

Living the Word

In our community the churches work together to raise money to distribute to those who are in need. Some people who seek assistance for gas or food promise to pay the money back later (it never happens). Most just receive it as a gift and then go on their way.

We don't give out cash, but we do send people to the gas station or grocery store, where we can pre-authorize the purchases by way of phone. One day a man told me he was in desperate need of assistance for both gas and food. I had never seen him before, but he seemed sincere. He said he had several children he needed to feed, including a baby in diapers. So we gave him some canned goods from the food pantry, sent him to the grocery store to get milk and other essentials, and finally sent him to the gas station to fill up.

When he got to the gas station, he filled up and signed the receipt to put the bill on the church's gas card. He didn't realize, though, that the man behind him in line was from the church. If he had, maybe he wouldn't have pulled all that cash out of his wallet to buy a bunch of lottery tickets. The church member was upset that we had helped a guy who had money in his wallet for lottery tickets, so he made a beeline to the church office to tell me. I listened to him complain for a while about how we should not be helping people who "do not deserve our help." I eventually asked him how I should sort out who deserves help and who doesn't.

I assured him that I understood his anger at being taken advantage of, but I told him that I was also sure that it happens far more often than just this one case. At that, his eyes got a little wider. "In fact," I continued honestly, "I'm pretty sure that the vast majority of people who come in here for help probably wouldn't deserve it if we look carefully enough at their life and spending habits." I went on to explain that the church is here to help people whether we think of them as "deserving" or not. I said that I thought we should be especially sure to help people who do not deserve our help, since that is the most accurate expression of the gospel message.

I don't think he liked my answer. But he got a glimpse from his judge's seat of people he does not usually get to see. Yet God sits in the judgment seat all the time. The thing is, I don't think that God watches only poor people who fritter their money away on lottery tickets or cigarettes or alcohol. I mean, really! Is God going to throw that man into hell for buying lottery tickets after using the church's handout, but overlook people who have three-car garages and many other luxuries, while thousands of people starve to death every day—and then do nothing at all about that? Do we really want a God who wants to help only the "deserving"? If so, in God's sight, then, are you "deserving" of all the things God has given and will give you? Then congratulations—you have earned what you have received! But many people, if God looks closely enough, might be found "undeserving." For example, what if God watches our thoughts while we stand behind another person in a checkout line? What if God knows whether we have stood in judgment of our brother? What if God keeps tabs on gossip, or lustful thoughts, or white lies? Our only hope is that God, the all-seeing, all-knowing judge of all, is willing to help the undeserving.

Let us pray:
Lord, thank you for forgiving us our sins, and for choosing to save those of us who are not deserving of your salvation. Help us have the same grace upon others. In Christ, Amen.

SUGGESTED PSALM: *Psalm 1*

SUGGESTED HYMNS:
  "My Hope Is Built" (B, C, F, L, P, UM)
  "Hope of the World" (E, F, P, UM, W)

Justified by Faith

Hearing the Word

The theme that links today's devotional scripture (2 Corinthians 3:4-11) to the lesson scripture (Romans 5:1-11, 18-21) is the new covenant. Paul wrote both of these books. In 2 Corinthians Paul contrasts the way of obedience to the law, which results in death (since we cannot keep it, and it only serves to highlight our sinfulness), with the way of the Spirit, which results in life. One is written on stone tablets (referring to Moses receiving the Ten Commandments; see Exodus 19–20), the other is written on the heart. One is imposed from the outside, but the other is internalized.

Living the Word

A man whose house had been nearly destroyed by a hurricane decided to hire a teenage boy to help him repair it. The man wanted to move back in it as soon as possible; the boy just wanted five dollars an hour so he could buy some music albums.

The man would frequently get up before dawn, and by the time the sun was coming up he would be out on the job site pulling nails out of salvageable boards, stacking lumber, or carrying old insulation, shingles, and other junk to the trash. Everywhere he looked he could see work to do. The thing that mystified him was that the boy would come and stand around, even after the time clock was running. He would ask, "What do you want me to do?" Sometimes the man would answer, "Just look around; there's plenty to do." Then later he would see the boy taking a break, sitting on a pile of lumber and listening to music on his headphones. Finally, the man fired him.

The difference between these two illustrates Paul's point in

61

2 Corinthians when he compares the law to life in the Spirit. The man was motivated to get the site cleaned up; it was something he wanted to do, so he naturally did the things that helped accomplish that purpose. He had the inward desire, the motivation, the "spirit" to do the work. The boy, on the other hand, was just trying to do whatever he had to do to get his money. He worked when directly told what to do, but even then he had no enthusiasm for it. He had no initiative; he could look around and not identify a task that needed to be done.

In much the same way, the crowd that received the Ten Commandments did not throw much of a party afterward. (They were afraid of Moses and of God.) In this way, they were like the teenager in the story above. Laws are usually restrictive in some way. They prevent us from doing something we otherwise might. For example, if we obey the rules of the road, we are not supposed to go faster than the speed limit; but without the law we might choose to go faster than that. Most people don't celebrate giving up some of their freedom. On the contrary, many people resist the law just like the teenager did; if they obey it they drag their feet, wait to be told exactly what to do, and so on. There is not a lot of joy in it. That is the old way of relating to God. God was the lawgiver, and we were the reluctant teen whose heart was not in it. Paul says that the old way did not work to save us—it only led to death.

However, the new covenant is different. It is represented by the man in the story above. He was a self-starter. Instead of being told what to do, he looked around and saw what needed to be done—and he *wanted* to do it! When we have the Spirit of Christ, as Paul points out, we change inwardly. We are motivated from within, not just restricted from without. In a sense, we become part of God's team because our relationship with God has been changed by Christ. No longer must we tug in the opposite direction. Instead, the Spirit of Christ in us does more than simply make us want to obey God's will, but changes us so that the rules are our will, too.

Let us pray:
Lord, thank you for instilling the desire in our hearts, through the Spirit of Christ, to live as you would have us live. Forgive us when our human nature still gets in the way, and we fall short. Help us live by what we affirm with our heart, your holy and pure life in Christ, Amen.

READ IN YOUR BIBLE: *Romans 6:15-23* March 27, 2005
SUGGESTED PSALM: *Psalm 100*
SUGGESTED HYMNS:
 "Christ the Lord Is Risen Today" (All)
 "The Strife Is O'er, the Battle Done" (B, E, L, P, UM, W)

Victory over Death

Hearing the Word

Paul begins Romans 6:15-23 with a question that is nearly identical to the question that begins today's lesson scripture (Romans 6:1-14, plus the resurrection account in John 20). The question asks whether we can continue to live in sin, since we are covered by God's grace anyway. The answer is a strong "no!" The reason is that our change to living under God's grace is like the death and resurrection of Jesus. We have died to sin and have come back to life with Christ. Thus the resurrection does even more than carry with it the promise of life after death. It has spiritual and personal implications for us here and now.

Living the Word

I saw an Easter cartoon that pictured two chocolate Easter bunnies, the hollow kind. Their yellow candy eyes were looking at each other. The first Easter bunny says, "Happy Easter!" The other bunny replies, "What?" Unfortunately, his ears, which are the favorite first target for most kids, had already been bitten off.

My sense of humor may have been a little zany, but perhaps the cartoon struck a chord with me because at the time I received it I was sitting down at my computer, staring at a blank page, trying to think of something inspirational to write. And I was getting desperate.

The cartoon reminded me of scurrying about as we clergy do this busy time of year, much like a rabbit, trying to create worship services and share inspirational messages for Maundy Thursday, Good Friday, Easter sunrise, and then the biggest service of the year—the one where you see some people in church only on this one occasion each year—Easter Sunday.

In the church, we do have an important and inspirational message to share with others. The content of our message for the world is deeper than "Happy Easter" of course. At the core of our message is "Jesus is risen, and because of that you can live a new life!" Paul wanted to make the point that the change in us from slaves of sin to slaves of righteousness is just as dramatic as the change from death to life. Not only that, the change results in the difference between death and life for us. When we come to Christ, it is a spiritual resurrection.

But the message can be overwhelmingly difficult to proclaim in a world like ours. Sometimes it feels like we are speaking to people whose ears, like the Easter bunny's were, are already bitten off. "What?" is not such an uncommon answer to Easter. Even the disciples said something like "What?" when they first heard that Jesus was raised from the dead.

Easter is a difficult message to understand and live out, even for those of us with ears. It is not easy to face death, especially the death of a loved one, and still affirm "Jesus is risen." And with the destruction that wars and terrorists seem to bring our way in this dangerous world, it is a challenge to still firmly believe that God is able to bring about new life no matter what. But that is what our faith tells us.

Certainly many in the world today, if they hear our message, will wonder what it means for them, and especially what Easter means for the worst circumstances of their life. If the church was ever faced with a time when our message "Jesus is risen" was vital and needed, it is today. If there was ever a time when people needed to hear our reason for hope, our faith in God's ability to create new life even out of death, then it is now. And if they ask "What?" we will just need to find another way to share the good news.

For we believe that God's love is stronger than death, and that no tomb, no matter how terrifying and bleak, could ever separate us from the love of God shown in the risen Lord of life, Jesus Christ.

May the good news of Easter soak into your spirit and change your life. It is truly the best news we will ever hear.

Let us pray:
Lord, thank you for the hope for eternal life that we have because of the resurrection of Jesus Christ. As we put our faith in you, may the sinful ways in us die forever, and may the joy and hope and faith of following Jesus Christ be like a resurrection within us. Amen.

SUGGESTED HYMNS:
  "My Hope Is Built" (B, E, F, L, P, UM)
  "Lift Every Voice and Sing" (B, E, L, P, UM, W)

Power for Living

Hearing the Word

In Romans 7:1-6, today's devotional scripture, Paul compares the effect of death on the legal requirements of marriage to our death to sin. Just as wedding vows and responsibilities pertain to a person as long as that person lives but end when that person dies, so it is when we enter into a new relationship with Christ—we "die" to the old "marriage" to sin. The old relationship only leads to death, but our new relationship with Christ leads to life. This discussion takes place in the midst of one of Paul's most lengthy and brilliant theological statements. The lesson scripture for the day (Romans 8) continues explaining the difference between life under the law (which leads to death) and the life of the Spirit (which leads to eternal life).

Living the Word

Last year we purchased a "farmette" as a potential place to retire. The house is fine, but one of the most special parts of the property to us is the old barn. Built in 1912, it is unusual; its huge windows on each exposure are made up of literally hundreds of five-inch panes of glass.

A church member showed us a picture of the barn taken in 1915. The barn has changed a lot since then. The grand old cupola has fallen off, and the roof now sags and leaks. The wood plank siding, new and straight in the photo, has now weathered. Most of the paint is gone. In addition, the gutters are rusty, leaking, or missing altogether. The photograph of that proud old barn shows all the windows in place, but now several panes of glass are missing, others rattle precariously in place, and some of the sills have rotted out, leaving whole window frames dangling by old rusty nails on the top side.

That barn was made to be a real showplace, but time takes its toll on barns. One person suggested that we tear it down; for the price of reroofing it we could build a small, cheap metal building in its place. There is a certain logic to that. But it is precisely these old characteristics that fascinate us; like many of the barns in our area, they embody a slice of history that deserves a new life today. We are not preserving our barn to make a museum out of it; rather, we plan to give it a new life as an actively used building—a woodworking shop, an art studio, or who knows.

The work of restoration reminds me of the Easter season. Paul writes that in our old relationship to the law, sin leads to death. A little lie here, a bit of gossip there are like rain showers on barn siding. You cannot see any difference after any one rain, but over the years the weather destroys the paint, weathers the siding boards, and eventually begins to rot out the inner structure. Sin is like that. Like the rain that rots the wood from the inside, our resentfulness, grudges, and hostility rot the good that God wants us to be filled with, leaving us with a paper-thin veneer of what we should be, but destroyed on the inside. Day by day sin weakens the whole structure; under the law we too are headed most certainly to death, like the barn was destined to become a heap of boards in the middle of the field.

Happily, there is another chance. God is in the restoration business, and we, like deteriorating old barns helpless to fight off the elements, need the restoring power of God's love and mercy. It is like the beginning of a new marriage, except that this relationship with God leads to life instead of death under the law. So in this new relationship of grace, even physical death itself cannot stop God from restoring us to new life. God will never give up on us—there is never so much of a mess, so much destruction, that God says, "Oh, it is better to just give up on that one and put another in its place." Thanks be to God, who is stronger than the elements of both sin and death.

Let us pray:
Lord, thank you for your restoring power, which can replace the deadly effects of sin with your good gift of life. Grant us new faith and hope as we celebrate what you have done for us through Jesus Christ, our risen Lord. Amen.

SUGGESTED PSALM: *Psalm 110*

SUGGESTED HYMNS:

"Come Down, O Love Divine" (E, L, P, UM, W)

"Love Divine, All Loves Excelling" (All)

Affirming Christ as Lord

Hearing the Word

One of the unique themes in Hebrews is the comparison of Jesus to a high priest. Probably this was unusual because the Jewish leaders were enemies of Jesus in his lifetime. However, the high priest did play a vital role in the Jewish community as the mediator between people and God. In that way, the comparison with Jesus is natural. The particular high priest mentioned repeatedly in Hebrews is Melchizedek. The reference in today's devotional scripture comes from Psalm 110:4, which unfortunately does not help us at all in understanding any of the details about him. The only other place in the Bible that mentions him is Genesis 14:17-24, where he blesses Abram after a victory. Perhaps when the book of Hebrews was written there was more commonly known about Melchizedek and why Jesus would have been compared to him, but much of that information must has been lost over time.

Living the Word

Labor representatives sit on one side, and management representatives sit on the other. They exchange glances and pleasantries, but after countless hours of talks over many days, they have been unable to resolve their differences. A strike is imminent. Finally, in walks a professional negotiator. He is not part of either side, but he is able to fully understand the needs of both sides and to help them establish a relationship they can live with. This is an example of one priestly function—to help restore a broken relationship.

Consider another analogy. A youth is arrested in a department store parking lot, suspected of stealing a CD. He is from a poor family. A public defender is appointed to represent the boy. The public defender makes a few phone calls and arranges for the boy to be released on bail. Then, when the court date arrives, the public defender approaches the judge and speaks on behalf of the boy, pleading his case. This is an example of another priestly function—that boy needed a representative to give him access to the system and to gain a fair hearing.

Consider yet another analogy. One of the fascinating sites on the Internet (www.Koko.org) documents the long relationship between Francine "Penny" Patterson, who holds a Ph.D. in developmental psychology from Stanford, and Koko, a gorilla that knows over one thousand different words in human sign language and responds to over two thousand different spoken words in English. The research Dr. Patterson is doing, along with her associates, provides a rare opportunity for interspecies communication. In this way, she serves as an intermediary between the world of humans and the world of gorillas. Notice another priestly function—a representative of one group (humans) who has a special relationship with the other (God). The result of this relationship is to reveal to the rest of us, through sermons and other spoken words, something about God.

Protestants are used to the thought that we have direct access to God and don't need an intermediary. But Hebrews makes the point that Jesus is our high priest. Through Christ, we have access to the system, much like the lawyer who represents a client. Christ has also sought and brought about restoration of a broken relationship between God and humanity through his sacrificial death on the cross; in this way Christ is similar to the professional negotiator (though even that analogy falls short of the fullness of what Christ has done for us). Finally, Christ was both 100 percent human and 100 percent divine. When we see Christ, we are looking at God, too. That way we know that our high priest lowered himself to experience our everyday mortal struggles. When we have a problem or worry and we talk to God about it, God is not some distant spiritual mist. No, God is able to nod knowingly when we pray, and says, "Yes, I've been there before."

Let us pray:
Lord, thank you for Jesus Christ, our representative, our mediator, our friend, and our Savior. Help us learn more of Jesus Christ, that we may come to know you and your will better in our life. Through Christ we pray, Amen.

SUGGESTED PSALM: *Psalm 133*

SUGGESTED HYMNS:

"Let Us Break Bread Together" (B, E, F, L, P, UM, W)

"O Master, Let Me Walk with Thee" (B, C, E, F, L, P, UM)

Living the Christian Life

Hearing the Word

Today's background scripture is Romans 12, which is a collection of diverse teachings that are lumped together under the general idea of living out the Christian life. These specific short teachings range from how to deal with people who persecute you to the evils of being lazy. The devotional text is one part of this chapter, verses 3-8, which deal with the different parts of the body living in harmony as one (compare it with 1 Corinthians 12 in which Paul deals with the idea in more length).

Living the Word

There is an old proverb that says, "When the toe hurts, the whole body bends." It is one way to express the fact that the human body consists of many parts, but even those that we might think are more humble, such as a toe, are still important enough that the whole body will pay attention if it is hurting.

To illustrate the idea that the body consists of many parts, and that they are each important and need to work together, a youth Sunday school curriculum had an experience in it for the youth to try (don't try this at home!). One person in the class had to wear a blindfold. That person could do anything, except he or she was not allowed to see. Likewise, another person had to sit in a chair and was not allowed to use his or her legs. Another person had to wear earphones with music playing and could not be allowed to hear what anyone else said. Another person had to wear handcuffs, and could not use his or her hands. Another person was not allowed to speak.

The students had to complete several simple tasks together such as sharpen a pencil, get a drink of water, go outside and take a walk, wash their hands in the restroom, and so on. Those who were unable to do a certain task were to be helped by those who could help them. The point was quickly made clear to the class. They each had gifts to give, but they also had needs that others could fill, so they needed each other.

This is the way it is in the church. One way or another, God usually provides someone who can play the organ or piano or guitar or sing in a praise band. But not everyone can do that! Some people know how to unravel all the requirements for payroll and filling out government forms for the church's employees. Some people can do a good job cleaning up the church, while others would step right over an overflowing trashcan without noticing it. Some can preach, some can teach, some are good listeners.

Probably one thing that churches tend to do is miss out on some of the gifts their members have to offer. Sometimes churches get in a rut and miss the opportunity to make use of a new person's gifts. For example, I can recall one church where we had trouble finding organists. Then we received a new family. It took five years before anyone realized that the mother of that family was able to play the piano. She was just waiting to be asked and didn't want to intrude. Another church held Vacation Bible School in the mornings and in the basement every year. Yet the best event they ever had was the year a church member secured a large tent, and a team of men put it up on the church lawn. Then we held the event in the evenings, and suddenly kids (and extra adults) from all over town wanted to be in the tent, and the Bible school just had a whole different feel to it. Some people taught, some put up the tent, some made refreshments, some did crafts, and some brought in bales of straw to sit on. As the children sat around on the bales of straw singing songs (one side jumping up singing/shouting "Allelu, Allelu, Allelu, Alleluia," and then the other side jumping up and shouting "Praise Ye the Lord!"), and all of us under the tent in the cooler hours of that hot August day, I thought, *"God, it is good that you have made the many parts in the body of Christ. We need them all, every one."*

Let us pray:
Lord, thank you for the variety of gifts that you bestow upon us. Help us find out what we can do, and be ready to contribute our part to the good of the whole body. Through Christ we pray, Amen.

READ IN YOUR BIBLE: *James 4:7-12*   **April 24, 2005**
SUGGESTED PSALM: *Psalm 145*
SUGGESTED HYMNS:
  "Blest Be the Tie That Binds" (B, C, F, L, P, UM)
  "There Is a Balm in Gilead" (B, E, F, P, UM, W)

Living in Harmony

Hearing the Word

In the verses of the devotional scripture, James seems to be addressing people who have been fighting and arguing with each other (see 4:1). The following verses, including the devotional text, deal with various reasons for conflict and/or advice about how to avoid it. The first part of the devotional scripture encourages humbleness (pride and boastfulness tear a community apart), and the second part (verses 11-12) caution against criticism. James is interested in the practical application of the Christian faith.

Living the Word

Charlie and Bob had been neighbors for years. Charlie was critical of everything that Bob did. "That's not the best way to clean out your gutters," Charlie would say, adding, "I told you the right way last year; why didn't you listen to me?" Bob could be wearing a brand new suit, but Charlie would only say, "Your hair is getting awful long. When are you going to get it cut?"

They sometimes went out hunting together, but of course Charlie had something critical to say even then. One day Bob bought a new hunting dog. As he trained it, he was shocked to discover that the dog could actually run across the top of the water. He couldn't wait to show it to Charlie. So one day they went out duck hunting, and Bob casually brought his new dog. He thought to himself, *"This dog can walk on water! Finally Charlie is going to have to say something good!"*

After a while, Bob had his dog retrieve a duck. The dog ran across the top of the water, got the duck, and ran back across the water. Charlie didn't say anything. Bob could not contain himself

71

any longer. "So, did you see that? What do you think about my new dog? Did you notice anything special about him?"

Charlie got a frown on his face, and replied, "Yep. That dog can't even swim."

If you ever want your words to be remembered for a long time, just turn them into criticism. When you criticize others, they remember it. Too bad that God doesn't have a remote control switch for our mouth like we have for our garage doors. When one of us got ready to criticize another person, God could push "close." Maybe it's better God lets us critique away. How would we live without criticism? How would the world continue to spin on its axis without people to tell others the things that are wrong about it? All of this is to say that criticism is a little more common than it might have to be.

Of course there are times when a child needs to be corrected, or an employer needs to confront a bad habit in an employee, or a citizen needs to speak up about something that is wrong. However, there are constructive and destructive ways to offer criticism. Here are three quick suggestions:

The first suggestion is not to do it. Just try your level best to be one of those rare people about whom, at his or her funeral, someone says "You know, honestly, I never once heard this person utter one word of criticism about anyone else." When you hear that comment, it usually means that the person had read James and decided to live by it. They thought to themselves, *Who am I to try to judge and criticize God's other children?*

The second suggestion is to offer positive help, creatively, when you see someone who needs some "adjustments." Nearly every potential negative comment can be turned around into a positive statement. When possible, it is better to say or do something positive instead of tearing down someone's ego. Praise someone until they live up to your hopes.

The third suggestion is to reread the first one.

Let us pray:
Lord, there are times when what I say is valuable, helpful, and positive, but perhaps there are other times when what I say is not. Help me learn to screen what I say using your values, that what I say may not bring sorrow to you or my neighbors. Amen.

READ IN YOUR BIBLE: *Acts 13:26-33*   **May 1, 2005**

SUGGESTED PSALM: *Psalm 63*

SUGGESTED HYMNS:

  "Open My Eyes, That I May See" (B, C, F, P, UM)

  "Take My Life, and Let It Be" (B, C, E, L, P, UM, W)

Hanging On to God's Good News

Hearing the Word

Today's devotional scripture is part of a sermon Paul preached in a synagogue, by invitation, in Antioch; this occurs near the beginning of his first major missionary journey, when he and Barnabas headed west to spread the gospel. The sermon goes through Jewish history, tells about John the Baptist's preaching, and then skips the life and teaching of Jesus entirely. Paul goes straight to the circumstances of the death and resurrection of Jesus, focusing instead on how it fulfilled the Prophets and why the people of that time and place failed to understand that Jesus was the Messiah. Of course, remember that Paul was not personally present for the events and teachings of Jesus, and Paul was interested in establishing that Jesus was the Messiah in the minds of his Jewish and Gentile listeners. This he successfully did; his speech was well received.

Living the Word

Recently I was asked to visit someone in jail. It was an eye-opening experience. The "visit" takes place right in the lobby by way of video hookup. There were only six TV monitor visiting stations available. Visitors look into a metal box at a five-inch black-and-white TV screen focused on a blank wall. The inmate stands in front of the blank wall for the visit.

With only one officer assisting, it became clear that visitors would wait in line. So I spent time getting to know the people around me. The mother in front of me had to drive across the state to visit her son, but when she got up to the table she was informed that one of

73

the prisoners in her son's cell block had given the guards some trouble so, as punishment, the entire cell block had their visiting privileges removed for two weeks. Suddenly, the mother began to beg the officer to speak to her son. "I've driven half the day to be here, and nobody let me know I couldn't see him! Can't I even call him?" No, ma'am, the prisoners in that section are not allowed any contact at all. "Can't you make an exception since it is his first time here?" Sorry ma'am, no exceptions. You'll have to come back in two weeks. She pleaded, "But that means I won't be able to talk to him until after Christmas! She left, upset and crying, knowing that her son would hear nothing, not even a message, from her this Christmas. She could not get her message through.

In talking to one of the guards, I expressed hope that the person I came to see would be able to turn her life around and make a change. He shook his head pessimistically and said, "Well, I've been here for years; I used to hope so too, but we specialize in repeat customers." He added, "What they really need is some good guidance." It seemed like he was telling me they really need the church, and I'm sure he is right. It's just that I was the only minister around, and there were a lot of people in there, and the only reason I was there was because I was directly asked to come. I found out that not many churches or pastors ever go to the jail to visit the people there.

Think about Paul. When he was in prison, he spoke to the guard and even converted him. Paul did not let any barrier or excuse keep him from going everywhere to spread the gospel. It's much easier, though, to just keep our message in the church; we're all set up there with our pews, pulpit, and sound system. But many of the people who need the gospel are not in church. So we must take the gospel to them, hopefully with the same zeal that Paul had.

That guard's comment spoke to me; it calls all of us to the difficult places where the message doesn't easily get through. So, will God's message get through to us?

Let us pray:
Lord, be with people who are in prison today. Help the church overcome the many barriers between our message of hope and any people in the world who need to hear it. Like Paul, help us boldly take your message to others. Amen.

Living on Faith

Hearing the Word

Paul's letter to the Galatians is a little heated in places (see the beginning of chapter 3, just before the devotional scripture begins). The main issue in the book, and what Paul deals with in 3:6-14, is whether Christians, after having been saved by faith, must also keep the laws of Moses in order to be put right with God. He cites the example of Abraham, who was put right with God by his faith, and Paul also argues that faith makes us true descendants of Abraham rather than merely biological descent. One of the early disputes in the church was regarding this issue; at stake, for example, was whether a Gentile (non-Jew) who converted to Christianity should have to keep all the food and Sabbath laws and be circumcised (if male). To Paul, such legal requirements diluted the fact that we are saved entirely by God's grace and our belief in Christ, and not by our human efforts.

Living the Word

One early morning, while I was still in bed asleep, the phone rang. When I answered it I heard an excited voice on the other end. It was a friend who had told us that she was expecting her horse to give birth to a new colt any day. She had asked us if we wanted to come see it when it was born, and we said that we did. On the phone she could hardly contain her excitement. "She's having her baby right now! Hurry! Hurry! Come over and see it! She's having it right now!"

There was a small gathering in the field—a couple of adults and some children, fascinated by the brand new colt laying in the dew of the early morning. "It was *just* born!" she said, "It hasn't even gotten up on its feet yet." One of the little children was jumping up and down for joy, hardly able to contain his excitement. Soon the colt tried to struggle to its feet. It looked a little like trying to balance a bag of apples on four walking canes. It wobbled like there was a hurricane blowing, but it managed a few steps. Finally, the colt simply toppled over—lying down gracefully was a lesson for another day.

It was one of life's sacred moments, to see this new mother cleaning off her colt as if nothing else existed or mattered in the world except that little baby. It was the gift of new life being given. And to watch that colt, which today could easily outrun any man, learn to take its first steps, was watching a miracle unfold before our eyes.

As that colt grew up, more and more would be asked of it by its human owners. For its early lessons it would have to learn to wear a halter, to follow on a lead rope, to submit to being tied to a stationary object. Later it would be taught to trot and lope, to side-step, to back up, or to rope cattle or pull a carriage.

In the future of that horse, there certainly will be many expectations that these owners will place upon it. There will be a great deal that the horse will be able to offer, but there will also be some disappointments. Perhaps it will not run as fast as hoped. Perhaps it will not quite have the form of a champion in the show ring, or the mental attitude that will make it a reliable work animal.

Yet no matter what the horse will offer, it will be fed and cared for all of its life. Seeing that newborn colt staggering around in the pasture reinforces the fact that the gift of life, and the sustenance of it, are not earned. They are a sign of God's grace.

I think Paul's point is that it is the same with us. God's grace is all we need to live and be sustained. There may be things we can do, and there may be disappointments too. But either way, we should not get confused into thinking that the only way we receive life in Christ is by our ability to keep the laws. It is the other way around for the Christian. We receive life and then, out of gratitude, we do the best we can.

Let us pray:
Lord, thank you for your grace, which comes first in our life. As we respond to your gift of life through Jesus Christ, may we seek to do your will. Guide us by your laws like a horse is led by the bit, that we may walk in your ways. Amen.

READ IN YOUR BIBLE: *Romans 3:27-31*   **May 15, 2005**

SUGGESTED PSALM: *Psalm 127*

SUGGESTED HYMNS:

"*My Hope Is Built*" (B, C, F, L, P, UM)

"*Christ Is Made the Sure Foundation*" (B, E, F, L, P, UM, W)

From Slave to Heir

Hearing the Word

Romans 3:27-31 continues Paul's thoughts about how God puts people right with God. As we have seen, Paul clearly believes that people are put right with God through their faith, and not by keeping the commands of the law (which he concludes is not possible for a human to do anyway). Reading between the lines in verse 29 and following, it is possible to see that one issue for the early church was that Jews and Gentiles were both being converted to Christianity, but their roots and religious backgrounds and cultural traditions were so different that it made it difficult to figure out how to integrate their radically different pasts with their new identities as Christians.

Living the Word

A documentary on the Discovery Channel explored the origin of one of the world's great marvels—the pyramids in Egypt. Apparently, the first known pyramid to be constructed experienced a partial collapse during construction, killing many workers and creating fear among the workers about working on them. The second pyramid to be constructed was being built at a conventionally steep angle, but for some reason, halfway up, the decision was made to lessen the angle and make the walls of the top half less steep. One reason may be that the bedrock was not sufficient to hold the weight, and so it settled. As cracks formed, it created the fear that another collapse was likely; therefore it was finished in a way to lighten the load and get done faster. Eventually the workers learned how to do it right, and in spite of the lack of modern tools, they were able to carve out gigantic blocks of stone and maneuver them into position so exactly that a piece of paper cannot be inserted in the cracks.

In modern construction, concepts such as level, plumb, and flush are important. They refer to the relative position of different parts of a building as it is being constructed. For example, if a concrete foundation is poured and is not perfectly level, then the entire building may lean, sag, or sit at an angle. Today's contractors would probably use a sextant; but imagine not having the benefit of modern tools and trying to level the entire pyramid, or make sure that the slope of the giant stones remained constant all the way up that giant structure. It was an incredible accomplishment to precisely line up all those different pieces so that they formed one new continuous surface.

This process of lining up the different stone surfaces reminds me of today's devotional scripture. Paul writes that "a person is put right with God only through faith, and not by doing what the Law commands" (3:28). The words put right mean to put in a proper place; we could stretch the meaning perhaps to include "to make level," "to make plumb," or "to make flush with each other." This means that our life needs to be brought in line with God. Paul could have said that the only way for that to happen would be for us to line up with what God wants (that is, obey God's laws to get ourselves in line with God's wishes). But Paul states that this process is accomplished not by doing what the law commands, but through faith. That is why, in Romans 3:27, Paul begins our devotional lesson with the words, "What, then, can we boast about? Nothing!" Being in line with God in our life is not our accomplishment; we did not do it by keeping the laws. No, we are more like the rock that has been picked up from a random pile, carefully fashioned by skillful and knowledgeable hands, and deliberately set in its proper place. We line up because of what God has done, and not because of what we have done. It is by God's grace that we have been "put right" with him.

Let us pray:
Lord, thank you for your gift of new life in Jesus Christ, a gift we could not earn for ourselves. Continue to work with us, like a stone mason who shapes a giant rock, removing from our life all that is not pleasing to you, and making us to come more and more in line with your will. Through Christ, our cornerstone, we pray. Amen.

READ IN YOUR BIBLE: *1 Peter 2:11-17*   **May 22, 2005**

SUGGESTED PSALM: *Psalm 25*

SUGGESTED HYMNS:

   "Stand Up, Stand Up for Jesus" (B, C, E, F, L, UM)
   "The Church of Christ, in Every Age" (B, L, P, UM, W)

Free to Serve

Hearing the Word

The link between the lesson scripture in Galatians and today's devotional scripture in 1 Peter is the freedom we have in Christ, and yet the duty we have to exercise our freedom responsibly. It is not merely permission to do anything we want to do. The letter of 1 Peter was written to Christians in Asia Minor who were undergoing persecution for their faith, and so they needed to be encouraged. In today's text, you can sense the "disconnect" between the world and the Christians who lived as "strangers and refugees in this world" (2:11). This is common for people who have given up, due to persecution, on the possibility of justice through conventional means or a good life for himself or herself in the world as it is. Therefore they feel like strangers, like temporary guests, and they are encouraged by the hope of a better world in heaven.

Living the Word

Reality TV is one more way our culture today is exploring the depths of human depravity. On reality TV shows, ordinary people seem to throw good moral standards and reasonableness out the window in exchange for the opportunity to gain a little attention or notoriety on TV. (I'm sorry to sound "old and conservative" already at the age of 44, but I was raised on *Gilligan's Island* and *I Love Lucy,* and so I am shocked by what I see these days.)

The Bachelor featured a man whose task it was to "sort through" twenty-five young women in a few weeks of dating to see which one he wanted to marry. He "dated" several women at a time, and near the end of the show, invited the last two contestants to an intimate evening in a hotel room. One of the young women went.

However it was refreshing that the other woman refused to lower her standards. She ended up "losing" on the show, but she "won" something far better than a bachelor who seemed to be forgetting all decent values: she kept her sense of right and wrong intact in the face of great pressure to let go of it.

Whether the media reflect our social values or shape them, or both, is a debate that can be left for another day. The fact is, however, that today's youth (and adults too) are faced with a quagmire of sexual depravity and a "value vacuum" on television and in the movies. Even in this day of AIDS, sex is often treated casually, like the big question is whether to have it on the first or second date. Virginity is either unheard of or ridiculed.

The young woman on the television show demonstrated a quality that the letter of 1 Peter wanted to encourage. She recognized that she was in a fantasy world on that TV show, and yet her life and values were still real and important. She kept them separate in her mind and did not get swept away by the culture around her. When the time came in which she was going to be pushed over the line, she knew where she stood and was not afraid to say no. That was both tough and admirable.

It is difficult to live as a Christian in a culture that does not reflect our values. Some people say that the U.S. is a Christian nation, and I do believe that it was founded on Christian principles. However, the culture today is not one that encourages Christian values. On the contrary, it challenges them to the core. As the scripture says, we are like "strangers and refugees in this world." So it is important that our "conduct among the heathen should be so good that ... they will have to recognize [our] good deeds and so praise God" (1 Peter 2:12). It concludes: "Respect everyone, love other believers, honor God, and respect the Emperor" (2:17).

To do this must be just as difficult today as it was when Christians were persecuted in that day. But it can be done. Just remember who you are, and where you stand.

Let us pray:
Lord, be especially with today's youth as they seek to find their way through the values of our culture to the values you would have for them. Help those of us who are adults to be models of good Christian conduct, like beacons in a dark night to help guide the way. Amen.

"Onward Christian Soldiers" (B, C, E, F, L, UM)
"Praise to the Lord, the Almighty" (B, E, F, L, P, UM, W)

Life Together

Hearing the Word

Today's devotional scripture comes from the First Letter of John
(most likely not the same John who wrote the Gospel of John). It
was written largely in response to false teaching that Jesus was not
a real person, and that to be holy required a person not to have
real contact with this world, since they thought this world was
evil. Therefore, the writer of 1 John stresses the reality of Jesus,
and the importance for Christians to love and care for other people. The link with the lesson scripture today (Galatians 5:22–6:10)
is that both stress the need to care for others.

Living the Word

During the war on Iraq Sanjay Gupta, an embedded reporter for
CNN was in Iraq covering the work of a military medical unit called
the "Devil Docs." On April 4, 2003, when a taxi drove through a U.S.
checkpoint in Iraq, marines shot at the vehicle. Two people inside the
car were killed instantly, but a two-year-old Iraqi boy survived in critical condition. He suffered multiple gunshot wounds, and needed
emergency brain surgery just to have a chance to survive. Only Dr.
Gupta had the expertise to perform the brain surgery that the boy
needed. So he changed roles from a reporter to a surgeon, and did the
surgery. Unfortunately, the boy later died, but the heroic effort to save
his life was both lauded and questioned.

CNN said they were proud of Dr. Gupta's actions and affirmed
that what he did was both morally correct and ethically appropriate as a professional reporter. They noted that even though some
people think that reporters should stay out of the stories and
remain objective observers, there are times when only the reporter

is in position to give life-saving aid to a person who needs it, and that takes priority over the task of reporting.

What better example of the words in 1 John 3:18: "Our love should not be just words and talk; it must be true love, which shows itself in action." It is easy to talk a good game, but what really counts is what we do. This is especially true when it comes to helping other people.

One of the hazards of being a preacher (and a writer for that matter) is that when we are working, we are merely putting one word after another. Words have their valuable place, and they can have a great deal of power and influence in the right settings. But when all is said and done, it is what is done that really counts. So it is one thing to talk about lonely people in a sermon, but real love is shown if you spend part of the day over at the nursing home or in the home of a person who recently lost a loved one.

James 2:14-26 puts it well. Verses 14-17 read:

> What good is it for one of you to say that you have faith if your actions do not prove it? Can that faith save you? Suppose there are brothers or sisters who need clothes and don't have enough to eat. What good is there in your saying to them, "God bless you! Keep warm and eat well!"—if you don't give them the necessities of life? So it is with faith: if it is alone and includes no actions, then it is dead.

How easy it is for any of us to talk about the poor and homeless, the hungry and the lonely, and shake our heads with concern. Likewise it is not difficult to say, "Aww, that's too bad" about the plight of refugees or those who suffer oppression. The hard part is to find a way to put our words into action. Real love can't resist trying to help, and is not content with empty promises. It is like a doctor who is asked to write a story, but when words suddenly do not seem like enough, then the doctor becomes the story. It is the story of love that has changed from word and talk to love in action.

Let us pray:
Lord, show us where your love is needed in our community, fill our hearts with your love, and let our hands demonstrate your love. Through Christ we pray, Amen.

Preparing for Leadership

Hearing the Word

In Matthew's Gospel, Isaiah 42:1-4 is important. It, or portions of it, appears three times, two of them the actual words of God at Jesus' baptism and transfiguration. These two events are key moments in Jesus' life and ministry. The voice of God that was heard at Jesus' baptism came just before Jesus began his public ministry, when he was "changing careers" from carpentry to being a homeless, wandering preacher. The second time the voice was heard was on the mountaintop at the time of Jesus' transfiguration—just before Jesus headed to Jerusalem to lay down his life for sinners. The third occasion that Matthew quotes these words is here in our devotional scripture for today. Matthew is highly interested in "proving" that Jesus is the Messiah by showing that Jesus' life fulfills the Scriptures (see 12:17, which is a common saying of Matthew).

Living the Word

One day a pastor got to church a little earlier than usual. As he passed by the Sunday school classrooms, he noticed a little boy sitting by himself in the kindergarten room. The teacher was not there yet, so the pastor stopped to talk. "Hey, it looks like you are all alone in there!" he offered good-naturedly.

However, the boy continued to look sullen. "It doesn't just look like I'm all alone in here," the boy answered, "I *am* all alone in here!"

The pastor wanted to cheer him up. "Oh, come on now, don't worry," he said, "I'm sure someone will be here soon to teach you and be with you."

With that, the boy looked up at the preacher. "Why not you?"

Why not you? That's a good question. All that boy needed was

83

someone to stay with him until his teacher got there. On behalf of that preacher, I'm sure he had a sermon on his mind and many other things. Sunday mornings can be a little nerve-wracking, and it would be hard to just change plans and sit in a classroom with one student making conversation while waiting on an absent teacher.

On the other hand, we all have our excuses at times, don't we? Sometimes we have just the right qualifications for the job, but we figure someone else ought to be the one to do it. You know the saying that goes something like this:

> Somebody had a job to do.
> Anybody could have done the job, and
> Everybody should have done the job, but
> Nobody did the job, because
> Everybody thought that it was a job that
> Somebody else would do.

It was a hard job, but "somebody" needed to do it. Today's scripture also includes the idea that Jesus was selected for the job (see 12:18). God had chosen Jesus, obviously, for his work. Jesus had to decide to accept it, though. The pastor in the story above could have heard "Why not you?" and sat down for a while, or he could have made an excuse and hurried off to the seclusion of his office to read the sermon over one last time. We don't know what he decided. We just know that the question "Why not you?" was posed to him. The response was up to him.

We probably do a disservice to God when we think of God's calling and selection for a task as something limited to career choice, particularly if we limit the idea of vocational calling just to choices we think of as ministry. The reality is that God calls us in ways large and small every day. Jesus heard a calling to leave carpentry behind, but Jesus also heard a calling in every sick or needy person he met.

Keep listening. You may soon be hearing the words—with your heart, if not your ears— *Why not you?*

Let us pray:
Lord, please help us listen to the ways you are calling us to serve you and one another. Be with all those who are serving you in the many different ways that you can be served, and help us all see new ways to minister in your name no matter what our vocation may be. Amen.

READ IN YOUR BIBLE: *Mark 7:31-37*

SUGGESTED PSALM: *Psalm 34:1-8*

SUGGESTED HYMNS:

  "All Hail the Power of Jesus' Name" (All)

  "A Mighty Fortress Is Our God" (All)

Healed to Wholeness

Hearing the Word

The healing of the man who was deaf and mute is found only in Mark's Gospel. The story occurs while Jesus is wandering in Gentile territory. The details of the healing are included because they are perhaps just as meaningful as the healing itself. The word Jesus spoke to heal the man is unusual; it means "open up," and appears to be uttered like a prayer. Even the detail that the word is uttered with a groan is given. Suddenly the Gentile who could not speak or hear can do both! Ironically, the disciples and particularly the Jewish leaders cannot seem to "hear" Jesus' message or speak it. To compound the irony, Jesus tells the people not to speak about the healing, but they do so all the more.

Living the Word

At a convention of preachers, I heard a talk about John Wesley. Apparently Wesley called individualistic Christians a "mere rope of sand." By that he meant that Christians who do not listen to or see the needs around them, and therefore fail to form bonds of community with other people, are like grains of sand. Even if they are shaped into the form of a rope, they have no strength because the individuals have not formed the "tie that binds."

After the talk, I went back to my hotel room. The cleaning lady was just going into the room next to mine. "I'll be getting to your room soon, Sir," she said. Still thinking about the talk, I replied, "Thanks." It was one of those replies you just make, not even noticing the person—almost like I was both deaf and mute. Besides, she was a stranger, and different from me in many ways.

As I pulled out my key to go into my room, it hit me—don't be a rope of sand! So I went back into the hall and said to her, "Excuse me." She looked up at me, and I said, "I just wondered if you heard about a guy that was in some sort of accident and lost his whole left side." She said no, so I finished the joke, "Well, don't worry.... He's *all right* now!"

She burst out laughing, walked toward me, and said, "Oh, God bless you, son!" That joke began a long conversation. She asked about the group that was there, and when I told her we were a group of five hundred preachers from all over Illinois, her face lit up. She said, "That's great! I got saved four years ago." She proceeded to tell me about her life and how her faith had put a stop to her drug and alcohol addictions. When she accepted Christ, she said God "just took away the hunger" to do those things. Now she said she is a different person. Her faith was obviously a blessing for her.

It was great to have the opportunity to get to know each other and share something significant right there in the hallway of the hotel. Many times someone who cleans hotel rooms would be "invisible" to us. We walk right by and do not see them. That is also true of the poor, the homeless, the prisoner, the powerless, the young, the old, the sick, and those with handicapping conditions, just to name a few examples. Can we hear their needs, or are we deaf to them? Do we communicate effectively with them, or are we mute?

Jesus healed the man of two things that prevented him from actively participating in his community—the ability to hear, and the ability to speak. Without these two things, we quickly become isolated, and contribute to the isolation of others. We become a Christian community that is best described as "a rope of sand." Christ can heal all of us of our deafness, so that we can hear the cries of the people, even the silent cries of the spirit. And Christ can also heal us of being mute when we need to speak. We don't always know what to say, but Christ can take even our lamest joke and our fumbling words and create a bond between two people, and with that true community is born.

Let us pray:
Lord, help us to listen to the cries of the needy both in our part of the country and around the world. Give us the courage we need to speak and share as appropriate, too, so that we can build bonds of trust and friendship and community between people. Through Christ, Amen.

SUGGESTED PSALM: *Psalm 55:12-21*

SUGGESTED HYMNS:

"*Break Thou the Bread of Life*" *(B, C, F, L, P, UM)*

"*O God, Our Help in Ages Past*" *(All)*

The Prevailing Good

Hearing the Word

Today's devotional scripture is set during the Last Supper and is found in all four Gospels. If you glance ahead to Mark 14:27, you will see that all along Jesus expected his disciples to abandon him; he also knew that Judas would betray him. The way he chose to reveal that Judas was the betrayer is significant. He didn't simply say, "It's Judas." He said, "One who dips his bread in the dish with me" (verse 18). They were all eating that way, and that meal became the forerunner of our sacrament of communion. Thus, Jesus knowingly broke bread with those he understood to deny him, betray him, and abandon him.

Living the Word

Our government put out large rewards for information leading to the capture of Osama bin Laden and others responsible for the terrorist attacks against the United States. The technique is exactly the same as those who wanted to catch Jesus; the only difference is that the Pharisees used the technique for an evil purpose. The question was whether anybody in Osama bin Laden's trusted circle had a price and could be "bought."

At the root, betrayal is a question of the strength of our loyalty and values. If money speaks loudly enough, then it will motivate our behavior. If our loyalty to a cause speaks louder than money, then it is that loyalty that will motivate us.

Some have speculated that Judas believed that the Messiah would lead true Jewish believers in a climactic final battle against the Roman occupying oppressors. Many faithful Jewish people believed that when this happened legions of angels from heaven would come help them fight for their freedom. Therefore, some think that Judas meant to create a crisis, to put Jesus in a position in which he would have to call in the angels and liberate the promised land. This is probably too charitable. It is more likely that he, like many of us, simply had a price at which the money became a more powerful motivator than his loyalty.

That is why he is a relevant case study for us still today. After all, when we read the story of Judas, many of us might think, "Well, what he did was wrong, but I don't have to worry about that because I'll never be put in the position of being one of Jesus' twelve disciples." We are like the other disciples that asked, "You don't mean me, do you, Lord?"

At the same meal Jesus predicted that Peter, who swore to stand by Jesus until the end, would deny that he even knew Jesus. He was a bold talker; but when it came right down to it, his loyalty was not as strong as his fear of the consequences of admitting that he knew Jesus. Further, the other disciples, like sheep without a shepherd, abandoned Jesus. They were loyal as long as Jesus was there to lead them, but when the going got rough, the disciples got going.

Whenever we lose our loyalty to God because of money, fear, or simple lack of direction, then that is a kind of betrayal and denial and abandonment. It is not that hard to make us lose our commitment to being in the "inner circle" of Jesus. We should be loyal friends of God, but instead money quite often gets our allegiance. We don't have time to serve on a church committee for an hour or so one evening a month, but we are more than willing if the boss asks, "Overtime tonight?" How are our values different from Judas or Peter's denial, or the disciples' abandonment?

Let us pray for loyalty to Christ, so that the clink of neither money nor anything else can shake our commitment to him. The good news is that Jesus already knew about the disciples' lack of loyalty and still dipped bread with them. They thought that he was talking about another, but he knew he was eating with people who needed his help, his forgiveness, and his love to be stronger.

Let us pray:
Lord, we confess that we find it hard to put you first. Forgive us for our lack of loyalty, or lack of commitment. Strengthen us that we may better serve you and follow you no matter what. In Christ we pray, Amen.

SUGGESTED PSALM: *Psalm 145:1-12*
SUGGESTED HYMNS:
  "I Love to Tell the Story" (B, C, F, L, UM)
  "All Glory, Laud, and Honor" (B, E, F, L, P, UM, W)

Hope in the Midst of Despair

Hearing the Word

The devotional scripture today is known as the Great Commission. It represents Jesus' last words to his disciples at the end of his resurrection appearances. These words do not only appear in all four Gospels, but they appear again in Acts. This is noteworthy because Luke wrote both the books of Luke and Acts—the only Gospel writer to continue with the story of the early church after Jesus' ascension into heaven—so it shows he considered these words to be of high importance. The link between the devotional and lesson scriptures is that at the beginning of Jesus' resurrection appearances (see the lesson scripture) and at the end of them, the disciples were given hope in the midst of their loss and grief.

Living the Word

I vividly remember when the "Jesus people" came to Decatur, Illinois, in the early 1970s. They fancied themselves to be the only true Christians in town, or so it seemed. It was during the years of flower children and hippies. Their services were held in a big tent pitched in a lot outside of town just about every night. But one Sunday morning the Jesus people came to our downtown, conservative church that was full of bankers, teachers, and professionals. The Jesus people walked down to the front and sat in the very front pew. They wore shabby clothing, put their feet over the railing like it was a footstool, talked loudly during many parts of the worship service, and slouched back with their hair dangling over the back of the wooden pew. Then when our preacher spoke, they laughed out loud at what he said. It was the closest I ever saw someone come to getting booted right out of the door by the ushers.

Of course, as a youth at the time, I visited "the tent" (as we called it) on more than one evening. They played rock music in their worship service, and the people all had their Bibles out underlining things during the sermon. I was embarrassed at the way they treated our pastor and church when they came, but I did think that they at least were making a genuine effort to "make disciples." If they wanted to stir up controversy, then yes, they did that. But the way they treated people on the street resulted in legal action, and I don't think that was what Jesus envisioned when he asked us to go into the world to make disciples.

On the other hand, I'm not sure we give that enough attention in many of our mainline churches today. For example, how many churches have a booth at the county or state fair? There may be a church that hosts a food stand; but instead of one out of a whole county, shouldn't most churches be finding a way to have a presence in a huge crowd like that? How about a water cooler with free water and a scripture about Jesus being the living water, plus a display showing the activities of the church, and brochures of the church to give away to everyone who would want one?

There are *many* other ways that we can reach out and interact with people we don't usually see at church. That was one thing the Jesus people believed in—they made their presence felt in Decatur, Illinois, that summer. Their techniques and attitudes were rude, pushy, and judgmental. But suppose a nice, loving, caring church wanted to reach others for Christ just as much as the Jesus people did. Do you just have to wait for potential new Christians to call your church during office hours, find out when you worship, get directions, and finally plop down in your pew? Or, can you figure out some creative ways to make a positive presence to everyone in your community? It's worth some thought, you know.

Let us pray:
Lord, remind us how important it is for us in your church to be seeking new people, and to make disciples. Forgive us for becoming more like a tight-knit club than a group that is intent on spreading and growing. Grant us the courage, creativity, and sense of mission it takes to reach out to others in your name. Amen.

Experiencing True Happiness

Hearing the Word

Matthew and Luke have a rather lengthy sermon of Jesus that occurs after choosing the twelve disciples and before the disciples are sent out on a mission. The sermon and other events between selecting and sending out the disciples could be regarded as a time of training. Matthew's sermon in chapters 5–7 is longer, and is called "The Sermon on the Mount" because it occurs on a mountain. By contrast, Luke's is called "The Sermon on the Plain." The Beatitudes at the beginning differ somewhat too, but the main points and the values of the sermon are consistent.

Living the Word

A newsletter article told of a little girl from a very poor family who was in the hospital. The nurse brought her a glass of milk, filled all the way to the top. However, at home the girl always had to share her food and drink with her siblings, so she had never had her own glass just to herself. The glass was still full when the nurse got back.

"Aren't you hungry?" the nurse asked.

"Oh, yes, I'm very hungry," the girl replied.

"Then I guess you don't like milk," the nurse wondered aloud.

"Oh, I love milk. It's my favorite drink—much better than just water."

Puzzled, the nurse asked, "Then why didn't you drink your milk?"

"You didn't tell me how deep I could drink," the girl said. "I didn't want to drink someone else's."

A tear came to the nurse's eyes, for she realized that the little girl had lived in dire poverty. "Honey," she said, "I brought you this whole glass just for you. And if you want more after you finish it, then here you can drink and eat until you are completely full."

There are also homes where older adults eat dog food because it is cheap. There are homes where the refrigerator is completely empty, and so are the cabinets. There are homes where, if you see anything edible, you would not want to eat it because the house is falling down, dirty, and ought to be condemned. And there are toddlers and children running around in that place.

The majority of people who are homeless or who live below the poverty line in America are children. In nations such as Haiti or parts of Africa, children are lucky to get a single bowl of rice in a day, and therefore many starve to death (the worldwide average is about thirty-two thousand hunger deaths every single day).

People who were sick or troubled or poor or weak flocked around Jesus when he preached. They all wanted to touch him, knowing that just a touch would often result in receiving his healing power. So Jesus began the Sermon on the Plain in Luke by offering good news to the poor, the hungry, and the grieving: "Happy are you poor; the Kingdom of God is yours! Happy are you who are hungry now; you will be filled! Happy are you who weep now; you will laugh!" (Luke 6:20-21).

The nurse in the story above reminds me of Jesus. She wanted the best for that little girl, and she was determined to make a complete turnabout in the girl's situation. Poverty, grief, and hunger will not last forever. Jesus announced that God is going to make a change, and it will be good news—like the chance to drink a whole glass of milk all by yourself, and to know that you do not have to be left wanting anymore.

Let us pray:
Lord, bless the children who must live in poverty in our nation and around the world. Be with the orphans, with those who are hungry, and with those who are homeless. Where there is danger or stress or grief or abuse or other threats, please make the day come soon when all will be well. And if, Lord, you need my help or the help of our church, make us part of your answer. Through Christ, Amen.

SUGGESTED PSALM: *Psalm 42*
SUGGESTED HYMNS:
  "O Worship the King" (B, C, E, F, L, P, UM)
  "Holy God, We Praise Thy Name" (E, F, L, P, UM, W)

Practicing Genuine Piety

Hearing the Word

The link between the devotional reading and the lesson scripture today is prayer. The lesson scripture comes from the Sermon on the Mount in Matthew; the section that is the lesson features Jesus' teachings on charity, prayer, and fasting, and the common idea behind them all is that they should be genuine—not done for show. In the devotional reading, Jesus uses the parable of the man knocking on a friend's door late at night to make the point that we should be persistent in our prayers. The lesson scripture includes the Lord's Prayer, and the devotional scripture immediately follows the Lord's Prayer in Luke's Gospel.

Living the Word

One small church I served had a family with three young children. They had apparently been teaching their children to pray, because in church one Sunday I said, "Let us pray," and began the pastoral prayer. I had gotten about halfway through the first sentence when their little boy, probably about age three, said out loud, "Amen." It was not too loud, but it was a small church, so we all heard it.

Being a professional, I knew it was important to continue the pastoral prayer. You know, they are supposed to be either long and boring, or boring and long (I'm kidding, but I'm sure some people in my churches just think I'm being honest). Anyway, I continued. I got another sentence out, and then he said it again, this time a little louder. "Amen!"

This time I could hear a few quiet snickers nearby, but everyone was still under control. The prayer turned the corner and went from thanksgiving to intercession, but suddenly there was another

93

"Amen!" This time I could hear his mother's vain attempts to keep him quiet, and other people's attempts to keep their giggles quiet, too.

I continued on with the prayer, but that boy was determined. This time he shouted insistently, "Amen!" I paused, and I'm sure his mother placed her praying hands over his mouth because now in rapid succession there was one muffled "Amen!" after another. You could hear "Amen! Amen! Amen!" through her fingers as her feet clomped on the wooden floors all the way across the back of the church and into the back room. But there were enough people laughing by then that I decided to add my "Amen" to his. It was a day I'm sure that mother will always remember.

Jesus wanted us to keep praying, to be persistent in prayer. In his parable, God would be compared to the friend who has already gone to bed and locked the door of the house at night. At first the friend in Jesus' story is not willing to get up to give the person (and Jesus brings the listener into the story as the person standing at the door and knocking) any bread. Jesus' point is not that God is reluctant. And God does not need to be nagged in order to be convinced to do something. Remember, this is not Jesus telling us how to manipulate God to get our wishes met. Rather, Jesus is talking to us about what is good for us. The story he told is really not about the friend inside; it is about us, and how to respond to our perception that sometimes the friend does not come to the door when we knock.

Have you ever felt like God just didn't answer one of your prayers? Prayer is not a heavenly vending machine, you know. It is a spiritual discipline by which we grow. It is a conversation with a friend. Jesus does affirm that God wants to give us good things, but this teaching is simple. Don't end your prayers with an "amen" too soon. Keep asking, keep seeking, keep knocking. No matter what the answers that come, it is simply good for you to keep praying.

Let us pray:

Lord, teach us to pray. Help those who are searching for answers that they cannot seem to find to hold on to their faith today. Guide us to understand prayer more as a way to draw near to you than a way to get our Christmas list delivered to us, and to be persistent in our lifetime about practicing this gift to our great good, and in keeping with your will. And now let all the people say "Amen!"

SUGGESTED PSALM: *Psalm 146*

SUGGESTED HYMNS:

"*Amazing Grace*" *(All)*

"*Blessed Assurance*" *(B, C, F, P, UM)*

Learning to Listen

Hearing the Word

Today the lesson scripture from Matthew and the devotional scripture from Mark are about Jesus' use of parables. In both Gospels, Jesus first tells the parable of the sower, which he expects the disciples to understand. However, they do not, and ask him why he uses parables to talk to the crowds. He quotes Isaiah to explain that the people listen but do not understand. The implication is that parables are something they can understand, then the double meaning will soak in later. Jesus goes on to explain the parable of the sower to the disciples; however it is interpreted there as an allegory (a story in which all the parts have a particular meaning, as opposed to a parable in which the various parts do not necessarily stand for anything, but the whole story together makes one single point).

Living the Word

In the middle of a stream are several big trout in an eddy near a rock. Their heads are facing upstream, into the current. The fish are not paying any attention to a fisherman who steps into the shallow water and ever so slowly works his way over toward the rock. Sneaking up on them from the downstream side, he slips his hand into the water and attempts to grab one. Of course he does not even get close. The fish darts away, and the others follow.

Grabbing his net, he continues the direct approach. "I'll scoop 'em out," he declares to nobody in particular. Chasing the fish upstream, he walks like a drunk man against the current on the slippery rocks, never getting close enough to the fish to even throw his net at them.

Eventually he notices another fisherman. This man brought a fishing pole. Soon he has his own pole and he puts a hook on the fishing line. He gets near the fish again, and this time he throws the hook and line into the water. The fish watch it go by, and show no interest at all. "Put some bait on the hook," the other fisherman wisely advised. "So the fisherman went back to the riverside, and this time he put some bait on the hook. When the bait came floating past, the fish saw what looked like a meal. It decided to eat the bait, and in so doing, took the hook into its mouth with it. And that is how the fish was caught.

Now what do you think this devotional has been about so far? It sounds like it has been about fishing, doesn't it? And if you like fishing, then it makes for some quick and easy reading. But really, it is a parable about parables!

You see, Jesus knew he wanted to "go fishing," and he used fishing imagery to tell the first disciples he called, who were fishermen, that he wanted to make them "fishers of men." Of course it was a little parable to help them understand what he wanted them to do. Out in the world we see people, but often they reject someone who sounds too "churchy." If they do not already believe in the Bible, then how does quoting them a bunch of Bible passages help to "catch" them? Jesus would have just told them a story (and not even explained it like I am explaining this one). He just told the story, and left it there. It made people curious, like a trout that decides to take a closer look at something floating by in the river. And if it looks good and is easy to swallow, they take it in, hook and all.

After all, there is nothing harder to catch, without a hook and bait, than a fish that is loose in the water. Just watch the grizzly bears try to catch salmon; they look so funny as they plunge and lunge and miss most of the time. But put a little bait on a hook, and the fish can soon be yours. People, like fish, don't really want to be caught. They will run away. But why is it that people run from what is good for them? Why do they resist the Scriptures and run away from God? That's a good question for another lesson. Today, it is enough to know that Jesus knew what he was doing. His parables have "caught fish" for centuries.

Let us pray:

Lord, help us hear your message, and receive it with joy, and share it with others in such a way that they too will receive your saving word. Amen.

   "Come, We That Love the Lord" (B, C, E, F, UM, W)
   "Lord, Whose Love Through Humble Service" (E, F, L, P, UM, W)

Free to Forgive

Hearing the Word

You only have to read between the lines of this letter to the Corinthians to see that the relationship between Paul and the church there has undergone some pretty rough times. Also, judging from 2 Corinthians 2:3-4, 9, it is clear that Paul at least feels the need to explain his first letter, and he may even have some regrets about sending it at all. There are a few people in Corinth who have claimed to be true apostles and labeled Paul a false apostle; this has created problems there. Paul shows a great deal of generosity and a forgiving approach even with those who have attacked him. He wants them to change but does not want their consequences to endure to the point that they quit the church; he wants reconciliation among all parties.

Living the Word

The church can be a tough, unforgiving place. It should not be—that is when sin has a front-row seat. A minister with small children made a parishioner upset. Unfortunately, the parishioner was the chair of the trustees. When the parsonage basement flooded soon thereafter, the trustee chair had all the ruined carpet ripped out of that level of the house, exposing the rough concrete floor. This included the living room and family room, the places where the baby crawled around all day. That trustee chair let the whole congregation and the pastor know that he refused to have the carpet replaced until the minister moved. It created a crisis; the leaders of the denomination in that area tried to intervene, but even they could not force the trustee chair to buy new carpet for the house. Of course there were other issues besides the carpet that made that place a painful one at least for the minister, and probably for many in the church too. The only alternative left to the denomination was to move the minister to a new place, but it took nearly three months to find a suitable opening. Worse, it gave the mean-spirited trustee exactly what he wanted—a new minister and a terrible dig at the old one.

The situation reminds me of Paul at the church in Corinth. We don't know all the details, but we know that Paul and his work was being attacked by some of the church leaders. It sounds like it was a mess. Paul could have washed his hands of it, or gotten the people to take sides and run the troublemakers out of the church on a rail. But instead—and this is remarkable to anyone who has ever felt good and angry with someone else—he worked for that person to be forgiven and to be accepted by others in the church.

When a group of people form a church, and if the church matters to them, there are sure to be conflicts and misunderstandings. For example, imagine a church leader resentful because she feels she has been carrying most of the load at Vacation Bible School. On the last day, when everyone is tired, someone makes the wrong comment. Suddenly harsh words are exchanged. Why? Christian people wanted good things for the children but had different ideas and expectations. Then the nail in the coffin is if they fail to forgive.

Maybe as you read this there is someone in the church who comes to your mind because he or she has hurt you. Maybe you still remember some harsh words the person said to you a year or more ago, and you still feel angry. Or maybe you sense that you have hurt someone else but don't know how to approach him or her. Are you willing to make a move to reconcile today?

One of the most difficult things to do in the church is to forgive. It is love's antidote to sin. Sin separates us like a wedge. It comes between us and breaks apart our relationships with anger and hurtful words, and the church is built on relationships. The damage can be permanent, and the church can become that rough, unforgiving place. But the evidence that God is at work to build up the church is the power of love expressed as forgiveness and reconciliation. So work with God, won't you?

Let us pray:
Lord, forgive us our sins, as we forgive those who sin against us. Amen.

READ IN YOUR BIBLE: *Luke 6:27-31*   **July 31, 2005**
SUGGESTED PSALM: *Psalm 70*
SUGGESTED HYMNS:
  "O Jesus, I Have Promised" (B, C, E, F, L, P, UM)
  "Take Up Thy Cross" (B, E, L, P, UM, W)

Meeting Human Needs

Hearing the Word

This devotional scripture continues the Sermon on the Plain (see "Hearing the Word," July 3) with Jesus' teaching about loving one's enemies. It includes the famous Golden Rule, which in Matthew's Sermon on the Mount is treated separately from Jesus' teaching on love for enemies. Depending on the context, it has some effect on the meaning of the Golden Rule; whether it is a general principle for how to treat people, or whether it is a principle to encourage peace, and more particularly to be applied to enemies. In terms of length, more than half of the Beatitudes in Luke's Gospel deal with the problem of people who persecute you. Jesus must have expected the disciples to experience rejection and persecution on their missionary journey, and so he wanted to prepare them. This section on loving enemies expands on the treatment of persecutors in the Beatitudes.

Living the Word

A high school freshman boy was getting picked on every day by a group of upperclassmen. Every day he had to go to the basement to the band room door to drop off his instrument before class. As he came up the long concrete ramp from the band room, the group of boys was waiting for him and would not let him pass. They taunted him and kept him down on the ramp, far from where any teachers were located, until the bell rang for class to begin. Sometimes they pushed his books out of his arms. One day they got him down, took off his tennis shoes, and hid them. They stuffed the boy in a trash can and rolled him down the ramp.

This boy, who was a recently converted Christian, had read the

99

devotional lesson we have for today: "Love your enemies, do good to those who hate you, bless those who curse you, and pray for those who mistreat you. If anyone hits you on one cheek, let him hit the other one too" (Luke 6:27-29). So he was trying to live out that biblical strategy. Unfortunately, in the process he was miserable and fearful every day. The bullies were not learning to leave him alone so he ended up talking to his advisor at school, because, after all, you can't go to class in your socks.

The advisor was a Christian man. The boy told him what was going on why he did not fight back. The advisor told him that he knew that verse in the Bible, but that it did not mean that Christians had to endure getting beat up every morning and live a life of misery. He said that one of the most difficult things to figure out is how to deal with people who would be our enemies. He pointed out that Jesus' teaching was an ideal, to show us that we should love other people, including our enemies, more than ourselves.

On the other hand, he said that you have to be smart about it. He pointed out that in the Civil Rights Movement, nonviolence meant that people did absorb the punishment from their enemies, but they had a purpose in doing that—they hoped their enemies would see themselves and see the error of their ways. In that way, they hoped to win over their enemies with love and without violence for violence. So, he said, sometimes suffering can have a creative purpose. But, he added, the Bible was not written to make Christians feel that they are so worthless you can just throw them in a trash can. You just have to be creative to overcome people who would be violent or otherwise be your enemies, he said.

So he arranged for an older high school student to escort the boy to and from the band room from that time on. Probably there were a few phone calls made to some parents, because after that the boy's enemies did not bother him anymore.

The boy tried to live out the saying "turn the other cheek," and nobody knows whether the bullies felt loved into being Christians after that. This is just one of those scriptures that is easy to understand and yet so difficult to live out in this world.

Let us pray:
Lord, if possible, please cause the bullies of the world to quit hurting people, and please help the hurting figure out how to love their enemies. Amen.

What Is My Calling?

Hearing the Word

Today the lesson scripture from Matthew and the devotional scripture from Luke are parallel passages; both are about Jesus being rejected in his hometown of Nazareth. Matthew's account is shorter and takes place later in Jesus' ministry than Luke's account, which occurs immediately after Jesus is baptized and begins his work. The event must have been a source of sadness for Jesus, since he would obviously have cared for the people in his hometown. In Matthew, the event comes just before John the Baptist is beheaded; this rejection of Jesus and then the death of John the Baptist, who came to pave the way for Jesus, have an ominous quality to them.

Living the Word

Imagine you are a teenage boy for a moment. You have been noticing a particular girl at school. She seems far too beautiful and popular to be interested in you, but then again when you see her at school she does say "Hi" in the hallway as she passes. You have thought about her a lot; in fact, all of a sudden the songs on the radio about love even make sense to you. When you find out that the homecoming dance is coming up , your mind is spinning.

That evening you sneak downstairs to talk on the phone in the computer room, where your parents can't hear you. You have brought the phone book downstairs. Your heart is pounding. Your fingers are actually shaking as you flip through the pages. "Why do there have to be so many Smiths?" You try one and it turns out to be her grandfather. "What do you want to ask her," he inquires. "Oh, nothing," you reply lamely. "Then what are you calling her for?" he says. But at least he gives you the correct number.. You dial it, and her mother answers. Waiting is torture for you. First you say that you are just calling to say "Hi." Then you ask how her classes are. "Fine." Well, that's good. Long pause. Do you like your teachers this year? "Yes, they're okay, I guess." Another long pause. "Well, I don't know if you'd really want to do this, but I was wondering ... well ... you know that homecoming is coming, and ... well ... I was thinking about going to the dance, and thought maybe ... well ... I don't know ... maybe you would want to go ... to the dance ... with me. So that's why I called."

"Oh!" she replies. "Well, I *have* been wanting to go, too. But there is this guy I really like, and he already asked me to go."

Can you hear the sound of his heart breaking? You have your hopes all built up, and you dream about the future, the way you would like it to be. Then the barrier you hit is not some understandable obstacle (like the schoolteachers going on strike); it is personal. The other person does not want the same thing you want. In that instant, you realize that your dreams are different. You have made yourself vulnerable by laying out your proposal, then it lays dashed on the ground dying a slow public death.

Jesus surely had hopes and dreams that his message would be well received, particularly in his hometown. In a way, he was most vulnerable there. It is where he had invested most of his life in relationships with other people. The rejection Jesus experienced in Nazareth represented his own people parting company with him on a deep, religious level, and even forcibly evicting him. It must have felt like the first nail in the cross to him, particularly because right after that John the Baptist, who was a step ahead of Jesus throughout his life, was beheaded. The two events taken together must have shaken Jesus to the core.

But in spite of rejection, Jesus went on preaching. That is the way to handle rejection. And trust God. For God understands rejection, believe me.

Let us pray:
Lord, help us in our life when we face rejection, whether it is rejection of something small or something that seems vital to us. Remind us that you have experienced rejection too, and yet you continued doing your work with those who would accept you. Help me to comfort those who may be stinging from the hurt of rejection, too. Amen.

SUGGESTED HYMNS:

"Dear Lord and Father of Mankind" (B, C, E, F, L, P, UM)

"Breathe on Me, Breath of God" (B, E, F, L, P, UM, W)

Hope for Healing

Hearing the Word

The devotional scripture today is a story within a story. The story of the woman who touched Jesus' cloak takes place when the story of Jairus's daughter is only halfway done; then that story is completed to end the scripture reading. The two main characters are quite different. Jairus was a Jewish leader, someone in the mainstream of Jewish life, and someone not afraid to ask for help. On the other hand, the woman was rendered "unclean" by her bleeding, and would have felt afraid to be found out touching Jesus because of her unclean condition. So while she had a silent hope, she intended to stay in the background.

Living the Word

Have you ever wondered how the decisions are made about who gets to talk to the president of the United States? Surely, there are more people who would like to talk than the president has time. There must be some kind of criteria used to sort through the requests and demands on the president's time.

Perhaps the decisions are governed by perceived political gains—those whose votes or money or support are needed are the people who get the president's attention. Or perhaps the president has a mission that mitigates the agenda of pure political gain—perhaps the president wishes to visit with at least one school child every day to get a child's view of the education system. If you were president, who could share a meal with you? Who would be blocked by security? Who would get five minutes of telephone time?

These kinds of questions are also lived out every day by other kinds of people. For example, United Methodist bishops, and church officials in other denominations, may have a policy to create a schedule far in advance. This means sorting through invitations to preach at a small church's one hundred fiftieth anniversary, and weighing that against the Council of Bishop's meeting the same week in another state, and weighing that against meeting with a long list of people who would like to talk to the bishop. The issue to look at is really one of access. Who gets attention?

I know that in the life of an ordinary pastor, sometimes it is true that "the squeaky wheel gets the grease." In other words, much of a pastor's time is determined by whoever is trying to get time with the pastor. That means two women can be grieving their husband's death; the one who calls and asks the pastor to talk probably will get more attention than the one who grieves quietly alone.

With the issue of access in mind, take another look at today's scripture. It contrasts two people who had different levels of access to Jesus. The first was a leader, a public figure. He needed attention right away, and he got it. But in the crowd of "regular people" there was another person who, because (1) she was a woman and (2) she was bleeding, was not allowed to speak to or touch Jesus. She tried to gain healing from the healer, but discreetly. After she was healed, Jesus insisted on identifying her and talking to her and giving her his blessing, too. He elevated her from a "nobody" to "somebody" important to him, just like the important leader Jairus.

In every community there are people who do not know how to gain access to the ministry of the church. It may be as simple as them not knowing the phone number or the times for worship. It may be a matter of encouraging and supporting the pastor in seeking out the more passive members and nonmembers or providing a bus to pick up the children whose parents don't make an effort to bring them.

But the question of who gets time and attention, and who does not, says a great deal about our real priorities and our mission. Who really has access to your church and its ministries, and who is out there thinking they aren't really important enough to deserve the attention, even though they are still in need of a healing touch?

Let us pray:
Lord, help us look closer into the crowds around us, especially for those who are passive and suffer quietly. Open our eyes to see their needs, and our hearts to show them the same love and acceptance we want everyone to feel from our church. In Christ, Amen.

READ IN YOUR BIBLE: *Matthew 22:34-40*   **August 21, 2005**

SUGGESTED PSALM: *Psalm 117*

SUGGESTED HYMNS:

  "Love Divine, All Loves Excelling" (All)

  "What Wondrous Love Is This" (B, E, F, L, P, UM, W)

Stretching Our Love

Hearing the Word

Matthew 22:34-40 is the famous question the Pharisees asked Jesus to try to trap him into saying something they could use to arrest him: "Teacher, which is the greatest commandment in the Law?" They wanted him to inadvertently speak against some of the laws by giving others more weight. It was a tricky question, but Jesus answered it in such a way that it showed his thorough understanding and analysis of the deeper meaning of all the laws, and his respect for them all. This is the third in a series of four hostile questions in a row in Matthew (the question about paying taxes, the question about rising from the dead, this one, and then the one about whose descendant the Messiah would be).

Living the Word

A funny story tells that an older couple invited a younger couple from their church to their home for a social evening as part of their church's "generation mixer" program. The idea was to help people get to know one another better across the generations.

The evening was going great. After a game of cards, the couples sat in the living room and talked about all kinds of things until late that evening. Finally, the women went into the kitchen for a few minutes, and the men were left sitting in the living room.

The young man said, "You know, I have to say that one of the things I didn't expect but that has really impressed me about tonight is the way you and your wife are so obviously still deeply in love after fifty years of marriage. I mean, all night long I have noticed that you still call her 'darling,' and 'sweetheart.' Tell me, what's the secret?"

105

With that, the older man hung his head. "I have to tell you the truth," he said, "I forgot her name about ten years ago."

Jesus knew that the secret was love—not just to marriage, but to religion. For all their knowledge about the many different nit-picky laws, the Pharisees did not understand the root of all of them. The underlying purpose of all the laws is simply for us to love God wholeheartedly and to love one another. Keeping these two create community and joy and peace. The absence of the love of God and love of neighbor leaves a trail of sin and alienation.

The Pharisees asked a loaded question. It was almost impossible to answer it without venturing into areas that humans should not—rendering an opinion about which of God's laws really matter the most, and therefore implying that certain other laws are really optional or at least unimportant. To speak like this would have been heresy to the Pharisees, and it is a tribute to Jesus that he saw through their seemingly innocent "sugar-coated" question to their vicious underlying agenda.

Jesus' answer was brilliant. First, he avoided falling into the trap of implying that any law was unimportant. Second, he provided a profound interpretation of the laws. He gave the Pharisees and other Jewish leaders an entirely new way of understanding the laws by detailing how to love God and love neighbor. He showed that he was the one who knew the laws the best, although he was not a trained rabbi. He went beyond "putting them in their place," though; his answer was still an attempt to teach them something vital about their own faith. In it you can almost sense a continuing glimmer of hope, as though Jesus was still hoping that they would change, and begin to see their religion less as a bunch of restrictive legalisms and more as a spirit of love.

They did not come around of course, but Jesus' insight has been a treasure, first given to his enemies and then shared with the world through the centuries. As Paul said in 1 Corinthians 13 (paraphrasing here): "I can be the most religious-looking and -acting person in the world, but if I do not have love, I am nothing."

Let us pray:

Lord, fill us with your love. Help us love one another and love you as you deserve. When our love fails, please forgive us and renew us that we might continue to learn from you and grow to become more like Jesus Christ, who was even able to love enemies and forgive sinners. Amen.

READ IN YOUR BIBLE: *1 Peter 5:3-10*   **August 28, 2005**
SUGGESTED PSALM: *Psalm 84*
SUGGESTED HYMNS:
  "He Leadeth Me, O Blessed Thought" (B, C, E, L, P, UM, W)
  "Take My Life, and Let It Be" (B, C, F, L, UM)

Building Community

Hearing the Word

After all that we know of Peter from reading about him in the Gospels, it is a treat that we also have two short letters of his in the New Testament. When he wrote, he intended to encourage people who were undergoing persecution, one of the big problems in the early church. In our devotional scripture, Peter directly addresses church leaders in the first section, and later he offers to everyone some guidelines that should help build up the community and strengthen their ties with one another. Finally, he assures his readers that God will help them through this time of persecution.

Living the Word

I like the joke about the preacher who comes to church wearing a bandage on his face. After church the people are in line shaking his hand. One man pauses and says, "I see you have a bandage on your face. What happened?"

The minister answers, "Oh, this morning I was thinking about my sermon, and I cut myself shaving."

The man replies, "Well, my advice is, next time you better think about shaving and cut your sermon!"

Being a minister is a little like being a coach. You get to make all your mistakes right out in public where everyone can see them. I remember one pastor who had a habit of repeating the words *this day,* which he emphasized in a churchy-sounding voice so often that it became like Chinese water torture. It got so bad that we would wait for the phrase to repeat over and over during the service. It was like waiting for those real loud "booms" when you are watching a fireworks show. Most of the fireworks are beautiful, but every once in a while your teeth rattle when the "boom" goes off.

So yes, with all seriousness let me say that I have a lot of sympathy for the people in the pew who endure, with the patience of Job, all the irritating things we pastors do, intentionally or unintentionally. I truly believe that laypeople deserve a gigantic pat on the back for all they do endure. Going back to the joke for a moment, just think how much more happiness (and time) there would be in the world if, when laypeople have heard enough of a bad sermon that is not getting any better the longer it gets, they could just say "Cut!" like a movie director. A lot fewer lunches would burn, too.

I want to add my "amen" to Peter's words in today's scripture. He wanted to encourage church leaders (this goes not only for pastors, but also for committee chairs, teachers, and other church leaders). Peter was a church leader himself, and if you read Acts you will see that it wasn't a bed of roses for him all the time, either.

To be a pastor, or a paid staff person, or a volunteer church leader can be tremendously difficult and stressful. Many people have their ideas about how things should be done, but it is truly impossible to please everyone. By now you have somehow slogged through all these pages of words from me, for which I thank you and admire you for your patience! When you close this book and are finished with it, why not pick up the phone or an ink pen and find one good thing to say about your pastor (remember that your other church leaders could use it, too), and give him or her a word of encouragement?

You might have to look hard for that one good compliment, especially when you have had to cringe through a sermon that has been both bad and long (they go together). But surely God put a little bit of good in everyone God has called to serve you. If you can look for it, find it, and then encourage that one thing, God will bless you. And through you God will bless your pastor (or church leader), and we will all know that Peter had an excellent thought when he decided to encourage the leaders of the church.

Let us pray:
Lord, thank you for those who have been willing to step forward to lead the church, both clergy and laypersons. Help us be supportive, helpful, and loving in every way we can, that they may be encouraged and creatively challenged to become the strongest leaders that they can be. Through Christ our Lord, Amen.